For

Mission Statement. My objective in this [   ]e, Jeremy Barnes, Author.

Your personal organisation skills will be vastly improved and more easily achieved through a simple self-training programme in time management, self-analysis, the setting and monitoring of targets and managing your projects.

This guide is a way for the student to get through their studies in an easier, more balanced and time effective way. In this book I am going to show you how you can organise your studies in a better and more controlled way. I will be dealing with your day to day tasks, your short and long term objectives and how you can achieve your final goal without the unnecessary stress related problems. It will be in straight forward no nonsense language in an easy simple step by step methodology, which anybody can follow.

At this early and crucial stage, you will be addressing the long term prospective of your career. It is essential therefore, and of paramount importance that in order for you to achieve success at the end of your journey, you firstly have to get properly organised. The skills you are about to learn will not only provide you with invaluable benefits in organisational skills for your studies but they will remain with you for your future career.

This learning will be of immediate value. The training is straightforward and simple to follow, it will not absorb your time, for as you will see, your skills will improve from day one. I can hear you already saying, "I really have no time to absorb this" The times I have heard this! Its a classic remark made by even senior management personnel, who, after going through this simple process find they do "work smarter" and, they never regret learning it.

The point I am making is, by improving your organisational skills you will be able to do more of the right work in a more controlled way with less pressure and in less time. You will be able to achieve your goals on time. You will remain focussed on the agenda at hand, cope with all the interruptions - good or bad - and when the crisis has passed be able to quickly continue from the stage where you left off. You will therefore remain motivated to your purpose. You will become more proactive rather than reactive. Being stressed out and de-motivated is the direct result of being disorganised.

In the past few years you have to some extent worked and moved in a more or less controlled structure in the way that you have studied. Organising your time and planning your work has not been such a controlling factor. It hasn't just been up to you as to when and how you study. You were driven by a certain procedure that you had to keep to and if you didn't, were guided in the right way and direction. Lessons were prepared for you. Homework was set within certain time frames and parameters, which had to be adhered to. Coupled with this, your parents organised your food, clothes, money and all the basic fundamentals of you life. So, to a point, your route map was planned for you.

At University it's mostly down to you! As at school there will be lectures, research, revision and studying to be done, papers to be read and written plus coursework together with *other* attractions or distractions depending on how you look at them. But the big welcome factor is you are free to pursue most of these at your leisure, or so you think! And here the danger lies. Because you have not properly analysed your workload you will assume (dangerous word) incorrectly, that you will be able to cope with it in the same way as you have in the past. With all this data to absorb it soon becomes a massive hill to climb, sometimes so high we prefer to make excuses and opt for what we think is the easy way around. We suffer from work overload! We fail to address the more pressing tasks by procrastinating until it is too late; leaving precious little time to catch up! What is the reason for procrastination? Edward Young the poet, informs us "It is the thief of time" Of course we conjure up many excuses both strong and feeble for postponing our work but the one fundamental underlying reason is, that we are out of control. We have not properly quantified the big picture, this is because we have no method or means by which to do so because we don't know how. We cannot estimate what is involved or even guess the time factors for research, revision, writing, study or even the order in which we are to approach the subjects.

The key is Organisational Skills. The danger of being disorganised is that we tend to squeeze ourselves into impossible time frames. We work extraordinary hours to catch up resulting in tiredness, mistakes and errors. We lose focus and purpose. Our decision making is pressurised through tiredness and the restraints of time. The resultant feeling is one of stress and de-motivation. Stress in healthy people is usually caused by their inability to organise their workload properly and they end up working longer hours than is needed. There is a way to deal with this. It's not a magic formula just a question of learning the right way in which you are going to organise your work.

To give you a simple analogy, if I said to you "In ten weeks time you will be able to jump a ten-metre hurdle" you would say, "it's impossible". And you would be correct, nobody could, but, if I showed you a way clearing the ten metres by jumping a metre every week, would that appeal to you? You see, the ten metres presents itself as an insurmountable task, a mountain, which is too difficult and too steep to climb. To you it is daunting and only leads to excuses to taking the short cut of going around it or avoiding it altogether. This is how University might appear at first, don't let it. View the course of studies you are embarking upon as a metre hurdle to jump every week. It will appear less formidable and far more achievable. How do we do this? By simply following the easy guide lines in this book and using personal Diary.

Ambition + Motivation = Goals
Ambition – Motivation = 0
Ambition + Dreams = 0

Ambition to succeed is the best motivator

The Author, Jeremy C. Barnes

I have held senior management positions with companies such as the British Aircraft Corporation, GEC, Black & Decker and with a large consortium operating in the USA. My work has been in the UK, USA, Germany and the Middle East. I was with the last company for twelve years as their General Manager and oversaw the company's operations in the whole of the Middle East. I was responsible for over 400 personnel. During this time I worked with managers, architects, project leaders, and commercial bankers in some leading multi-national companies in industry as well as the commercial side of banking. This experience has given me a unique opportunity to observe and learn the management techniques employed by a good cross section of personnel. In this time I have accumulated a wide understanding in management skills and an extensive knowledge of good management and organisational practice.

Over the past twelve years I have trained over 3000 personnel through my own management training company, in the art of good management skills. In the latter years I have specialised in one to one coaching of management. The personnel that I have trained have come from all aspects of business from top organisations both from the public and private sectors and, from a wide and varied range of vocations from managing directors, management personnel, and laboratory technicians, from doctors to people who run shops. This has given me a unique opportunity to study and observe the way in which they run their business lives. Without a shadow of a doubt the most successful of them have developed and use a certain technique in the way they organise and go about their business. Organisational skills should be learnt right from the start and that is the reason for writing this student's guide.

All the personnel I have coached and trained and without exception, their basic requirement I found was to have their organisational skills improved. Without good organisational skills it is very difficult and almost impossible to take on more work and responsibilities, without suffering a good deal of anxiety. The skills I teach are not usually taught at school or university and if they are, to no great depth as in a training course. So it is little wonder that the lack of organisation skills is extended deep into people's careers!

Over the past two years both my friend's children and my grandchildren have attended university, which in turn has given me a valuable and up to date insight as to what you are faced with. It has given me the opportunity to study and observe how they and others approach their studies and how they organise their new way of life.

Having seen the challenges that new students are presented with, coupled with the shortcomings of the way that professionals perform at their particular modus operandi; and the sure knowledge that they improved their output through my methodology, is the reason why I have written this simple and uncomplicated approach. The student will learn a way of organising themselves so they can approach their work and meet their forthcoming challenges in easy stages and in a more proactive rather than a reactive way.

Make sure the opportunity you have worked so hard for is not lost. I hope you find this book an inspiration for you to succeed.

Good luck.

Jeremy C. Barnes

University is the start of something BIG, don't belittle it!

THE FIVE STAGES FOR SELF- IMPROVEMENT THROUGH GOOD ORGANISATION SKILLS

STAGE I

TIME MANAGEMENT AND YOUR PERSONAL DIARY ORGANISER. Organising your time and dealing with time management skills. Prioritising and sequencing your day-to-day workload. Keeping track of all your work so that nothing is missed or forgotten. Keeping track of your cash flow. Monitoring data due from other people. Keeping records of all your appointments and holidays.

STAGE II

SELF-ANALYSIS. Looking inwards at one's own performance for self-improvement by identifying and focussing on the areas that you need to strengthen by performing your own self-assessment and showing you an easy way in which to do it.

STAGE III

WORKING SMARTER. A method of getting the right work done through working in a more proactive and better way. The economical use of your time in the way you work. Realising the true value and benefits of working smarter.

STAGE IV

TARGETS. Making targets constant motivators. Showing you how to identify and set your targets together with their end dates and a way to monitor them and show you a path to follow in order for you to achieve your objectives.

STAGE V

PROJECT MANAGEMENT. Analysing and breaking your projects down into modules so they are manageable and achievable by incorporating the steps you have learned in the past 4 stages.

What is Time Management?

Time management is a way of controlling your workload, studies, and leisure in a more balanced and less stressful way.

Time management organises your workload and puts it into perspective so you can organise and control your work by identifying the most important things to do and making sure there is time to do them in the day they have to be done. It also enables you to complete all the other items that are less important in the time you have allotted to do them. It puts your mind at rest by properly planning your daily, monthly and yearly schedules and targets, knowing they are all recorded in a place that will remind you to do them as and when the time comes. This will be a way of setting the milestones for your journey. Managing your time and work gives you the ability to change and adjust your actions and deal with interferences - good or bad - in a more proactive way. It keeps you focussed on the subject at hand and stops you from wandering from your chosen course.

Good time management gives more control over your life, as opposed to being controlled by other factions. The reasons for finding yourself controlled by others is because you have not properly planned your work and therefore have no argument or means to rationalise or to react positively to a situation or crisis when they occur. The general reaction to other's demands and distractions is usually to go with the flow and accept them. All very well but irritating when the distraction takes you away from the work you set yourself to do. And because of the interruptions you are working extended and extraordinary hours in order to make up for lost time. Lack of planning denies one the ability to say no! A good percentage of items that are supposedly urgent are simply because the person who should have dealt with them in the first instance put them off until it was too late. Courier companies have made a small fortune out of people leaving things too late. To quote one of my bosses "why should your lack of planning constitute a crisis on my part?" Your reaction to interruptions should be met in a more proactive way and should not be another crisis to deal with, thus leading to further procrastination and causing unnecessary stress.

Firstly lets start with the basic principles of good organisation skills.

There is no mystique in good time management. It is achieved through learning a very simple process and, of equal importance to retain and practice the process faithfully until it becomes a habit.

The process you are going through in organisation and effective management of your time will be like making a personal road map of how you are going to achieve your objectives. It will enable you to plan your route, establish its approximate duration by setting the signposts and milestones that you need to guide you on your journey. It will take into account and make allowances for, delays and the challenges of unforeseen hazards (managing crisis) and keep you focused on the main route leading to your goals.

The whole learning process has been set in five stages. Each stage has been designed to fit your work programme so as not to be a hindrance or isolate you from your own work. Therefore it will enable you immediately to incorporate your work in the learning programme by working with an actual work scenario and not purely by example.

STAGE 1: YOUR PERSONAL DIARY SYSTEM

"There is nothing more difficult to take in hand, more perilous to conduct, than to take a lead in the introduction of a new order of things, because the innovation has for it's enemies all those who have done well under the old conditions and lukewarm defenders in those who may do well under the new"

Machiavelli

The Prince
(1513)

As you see, there's nothing new in the grand scheme of things!

Introduction

Your chances of success will be greatly improved by being better organised in your studies and coursework. The aim of this book is to show an effective and straightforward procedure, in no nonsense language, of a methodology that will immediately improve your organisation ability and help you plan your studies and work in a more pragmatic way. The overall objective is that you achieve your goals, objectives and complete your work in a more controlled and less stressful way thus utilising maximum use of your time.

When you have learned these simple skills and practice, which will be habit forming, they will equip you with skills that will be of immense benefit to you for the rest of you life. This methodology will thus become an automatic and therefore unconscious skill.

It is all a question of getting into a discipline by learning a new methodology. I hear you saying, "I haven't got the time to do this! But it is better to stop and study the map and plan the journey you are embarking upon rather than keep aimlessly going on, and probably arriving at a place you don't want to be! By adopting this method you will arrive at your destination in less time and with less anxiety. These new skills will allow you to formulate the process of your studies together with the other important issues in your own life in a more organised and balanced way and, at the same time, not losing sight of your goals.

There is an old adage that goes "How do you eat an elephant? Answer "A bite a day" All very clever you might say, but it means that some tasks seem so enormous that at first they appear impossible. At sometime or other all of us bite off more than we can chew and it becomes indigestible. The message is, don't rush into something too quickly. Analyse it first and by so doing break it down into more easily managed components and completing one section within the time frame you have calculated and allowed for. How do we achieve this? Well it is all about improving your organisation abilities and showing you a method of quantifying and planning your workload.

At University you will be faced with a great deal of in depth study and large quantities of information and data to absorb. At first you will be overwhelmed by all the data and will probably suffer from information overload. How then do you climb this somewhat insurmountable mountain? I use the mountain analogy as a means of showing you that there is a way to climb or jump great heights, which may at first appear impossible. Let's take a lesser height, for example; if I said, "in ten weeks time you will be able to jump a ten-metre hurdle" you would think it would be an impossible task. Yes I grant you, it would seem impossible. But, with the right training if I showed you a way of jumping a metre per week, does that sound more achievable? Of course it does. So over the following pages I will show you a simple approach, which will instil a new habit in your organisational skills to enable you to take the large workloads on that you will encounter, so that you can deal with them in a more controlled and less stressful way.

Your diary and its uses

If you are already using an organisation tool, such as a manual or electronic diary like Outlook or a just a simple manual day-to-day diary all well and good. However, if you don't use either of these, you should start using a manual diary as a matter of some urgency. You may find the electronic method is inflexible for your use at present, but will find it of significant importance when moving into a profession once you have left university. I am not going to attempt to introduce an electronic diary because once you have mastered and got into the routine of the manual system you will fall into the use of the electronic more easily. Therefore, for the purposes of getting you into a programme of organisational skills more quickly, I think, you will find it easier to concentrate on the manual diary. Without the means of an organisation tool you will seriously jeopardise your chances of success.

First of all, if you have not already got one, get started by purchasing, a simple inexpensive manual diary. It has to have a day or two days per page with appointments, a year calendar and preferably a cash account column for every month. If you can afford it, a personal organiser would have all this data. If you search around there are some basic ones that can be purchased at quite reasonable prices.

The diary organiser is for you to record and monitor all your targets, appointments, daily tasks, note taking, retaining ideas by writing them down as and when they occur, tracking promises from others. Keeping account of your cash flow and keep fit charts and all the simple actions you wish to do even for shopping. This also will be of great help to you even if you use an electronic diary. What you want to avoid is notes written on scraps of paper and yellow stickers which can get missed or lost and most certainly will not communicate with you.

The reason for using a Dairy when used properly and continually supported is that the Dairy will "communicate" with you. Using a Dairy is a means of de-cluttering your mind of unnecessary information; it will keep your mind clear for your more important studies and issues. Committing an action in the written form is a safer way and will not be temporarily forgotten in the subconscious. Never think that you will become a slave to your diary, your diary will eventually become a slave to you.

Here are a few tips for purchasing a diary (your personal organiser)

1) *Make sure your diary has one day or two days per page.*

2) *It must be "with appointments" such as the hours down the left hand side of the page (see examples in the following pages)*

3) *It is essential to have a year calendar spread over two pages. (gives you more space to write in)*

4) *It would be helpful if there is a single page for each month to record your short-term targets and goals. (for this purpose, if you cannot find one with a month page be innovative and use the last day of the month?)*

5) *A cash account page per month.*

6) *If you cannot find this data in a diary try looking for an inexpensive personal organiser, they are to be found.*

In the next pages I am going to take you through a step-by-step procedure in a simple methodology and rules for running a diary. Each step will be accompanied with practical tips so you can organise your studies in a more proactive way. Practice these simple methods on a regular basis over the next few weeks and it will induce a behaviour change in you, which is an important part of the process for forming a habit, after that it will become an automatic skill.

Step 1 Stage 1

Organising your diary system: "The Calendar"

Calendar year overview. At the front of your diary (See example fig 1)

This is the first stage in transforming and customising your diary.

Mark in your calendar only the important dates that have to be kept and cannot be cancelled or postponed. (see below for examples) This will give you at a glance the big milestones that have to be observed.

- Birthdays, anniversaries and major event days.

- Rents due also fees.

- Exam dates etc

- Mid term breaks

- Term's start and finish dates.

- University days.

- **Public and Bank holidays.** Be <u>sure</u> they are **A)** correct to the particular region/country you are residing and more importantly **B)** your particular University may possibly work on those days, Scotland, Wales and Northern Ireland may have different dates and times.

- Motor tax or insurance policies are due.

Note! When recording birthdays or reminders for travel days give yourself a good margin of time in order to buy tickets, cards etc.

It is best to do these straight away. You want to avoid surprises of dates and deadlines creeping up unnoticed and sometimes too late. This eliminates committing to memory important dates, because once you get involved in University life, dates can and will be easily forgotten. Avoid highlighting with marker pens or a colouring agent, mistakes are difficult to erase, they look messy and will lead to confusion. In special circumstances like Christmas or the start of term, target dates or exam dates you may choose to highlight these, but be 100% sure that you get their dates right first time.

Hints and useful tips

- Use a pencil at all times. Carbon can be easily erased; pens etc look messy when erased and lead to mistakes and confusion with dates.

- Be proactive and not reactive in your planning.

- Don't forget only the big events for you calendar all the others will be dealt with per month as you proceed through these steps.

- A quick glance at the Calendar ensures you do not commit to something you cannot keep.

- At a glance, you will see what commitments you have as and when an extraordinary event or a crisis occurs.

- You may have to rearrange your daily events around a crisis, but this will still keep you in focus and aware of the big events.

- Avoid double booking.

- Avoid disappointing others, like missing Birthdays and anniversaries etc.

- Avoid conflict with your daily routine and others.

- Avoid having to re-schedule or rearrange tasks because of double booking.

- Keep to the big event dates, all the other ones will be catered for at a later stage.

- You may wish to highlight special target dates with a star or asterisk.

Fail to prepare, prepare to fail

Fig 1 Stage 1

Organising your diary: Example: Calendar found to the front of your diary

Booking your holidays and fixed dates

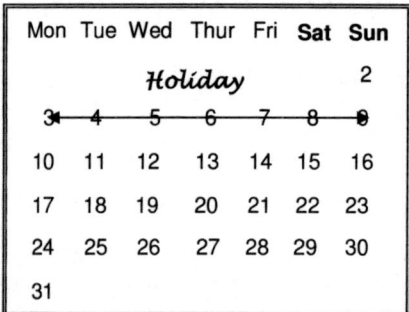

Mon	Tue	Wed	Thur	Fri	Sat	Sun
		Holiday				2
3	4	5	6	7	8	9
10	11	12	13	14	15	16
17	18	19	20	21	22	23
24	25	26	27	28	29	30
31						

Mon	Tue	Wed	Thur	Fri	Sat	Sun
	1	2	3	4	5	6
7	8	9	10	11	12	13
14	15	16	17	18	19	20
21	22	23	24	25	26	27
28	29	30	← *Mums Birthday*			

Month

Mon	Tue	Wed	Thur	Fri	Sat	Sun
			1	2	3	4
5	6	7	8	9	10	11
12	13	14	15	16	17	18
19	20	21	22	23	24	25
26	27	28	29	30	31	

Month

Mon	Tue	Wed	Thur	Fri	Sat	Sun
		Exams				1
2	3	4	5	6	7	8
9	10	11	12	13	14	15
16	17	18	19	20	21	22
23	24	25	26	27	28	29
30	31					

- Block only the dates that cannot be changed. All other dates are entered in your Month page at the start of each month.

- Try to avoid highlights

- Use pencil at all times

Step 2 Stage 1

Format for your daily diary page.

The following example is a typical day page you will find in a diary. It should have the times down on the left side of the page. So leave space to write your appointments, and leave a space on the right hand side to write down your things to-do, examples of which are illustrated with each step.

Against the times in the evening you will be able to record your personal appointments and to the right of this "due from others"

If you keep records of your fitness programme or want to keep records of accumulated points from the sport you do, then you can keep a space at the foot of the page for this purpose.

All of these are illustrated in examples, the format which, will be referred to throughout this book.

Diary Step 2 Example of how you can utilise your diary page

May
Monday 17th

Typical Diary page, with appointments

08.00		
08.30		Start to-do's from
09.00		right of centre
09.30		
10.00	Leave space for brackets and	
10.30	for sequencing your work	
11.00		
11.30		
12.00		
12.30		

18.00	Record "due from others" after 6pm	

"Exercise point gained today.........Means achieved.............................

Aggregate Points"...............

Step 2 Stage 1

Organising your diary: "Appointments"

1) Before you make any diary entry, transfer all the dates for the month ahead that you have written in your year calendar to the appropriate daily page.

2) Daily appointments page, hour by hour (left side of day page, see examples. This exercise should be done each Friday. When you know the lecture times and other appointments like dates for meetings, book their times into the appropriate day, bracket the complete period from the start to end time. Also from the Month page found at the start of each month.

Book times for following
Research, Reading/Library, Study, Revision, Writing papers, Doctors and Dentist appointments, Meetings, Leisure activities, Sport, Workout/Gymnasium.

Hints and practical tips

- *Use a pencil at all times, altering ball point is messy.*
- *Write in the locations of meetings or where the appointment place will be.*
- *Allow time to get to your place of work/study, lecture etc.*
- *Ever had an idea and then forgotten it, only for it to come to mind when you are either going home or to bed? This is because you mind relaxes and allows thoughts, ideas or things that we wanted to do to resurface. The way to deal with this is to get into the habit of writing them down as and when they come to mind and, certainly not onto yellow stickers. Write them into the appropriate place in your diary as and when you can do them and, if references are important, write down where to access them. Don't commit everything to memory. There will inevitably come a time when through no fault of your own, outside pressures and demands such as crises will divert your attention and make you temporarily forget or, put the thought out of mind. Your thoughts and ideas will drop deep into your subconscious and only resurface when you are least expecting them, and usually when it is too late.*
- *It may help to write down the lecturer's name and room number by the appointment, it minimises confusion when looking for the room.*
- Transferring your calendar dates first, avoids double bookings Keep transfers from your calendar to one month ahead. Dates and times may alter and throw off your plans. Remember, if a calendar date changes in the current month the alteration will have to be made in your daily page as well.
- *Always allow a time between appointments such as meetings which don't usually finish exactly on time. Furthermore, remember the next place you are going to may be some distance away so plan for it.*
- *Avoid highlighting, times and dates may change.*
- *Blocking off all you appointments will show just how much time you have left to do the other tasks.*

Diary: Step 2 Fig 2

Fig (2) *Examples of: "appointments"*

Typical Diary page, with appointments

May	
Monday	**17th**

08.00	
08.30	
09.00	
09.30	
10.00	* Lecture Room 51 Block C
10.30	
11.00	
11.30	
12.00	Lunch
12.30	
13.00	
13.30	Library (research)
14.00	
14.30	
15.00	
15.30	
16.00	
16.30	
17.00	* Gym workout
17.30	
18.00	
18.30	
19.00	
20.00	
20.30	
21.00	

Exercise point gained today...................Means achieved............................

Aggregate Points...............

Step 3 Stage 1

***Instructions in the use of your diary.* "Things to do list"**

Daily Page. Things to do list. (see example fig 3)

In general, and in order to get through the working day, most of us will make a list of things to do. The danger of having this list is that one tends to view it as a never-ending line of tasks, which is continually being added to and very little taken off. This list becomes a "no go area" a place to avoid rather than a plan for action. Tasks merge into each other and bear little resemblance to their true importance or the time required for doing them. One ends up by looking at the list and thinking, "I've haven't done one of these tasks" The action then is to complete one of them through desperation or conscience and choose the one that takes only five minutes but, it was not the most important one to do. This action in the very short term gives us a sense of achievement that will only last a very brief while. You end the day by putting off any decision making until the following morning. The next day you find yourself rewriting the list and starting the whole list all over again wasting even more of your precious time. This lack of organisation makes you reactive rather than proactive to a situation, you become a fire fighter putting out fires that you may have started yourself! The solution to this and a way to save time and ease decision making is to have a place to write tasks and ideas down when you know you that you can do them.

When things to do or ideas come to mind, write them down on the right side of the day page but, only on the day when you know that you have the time to do them. This will protect the time you have allocated from other demands. This is achieved by quickly consulting the left side of the page in the appointment's section to see if time is available, which will become obvious once you have booked your appointments. Don't forget to use a pencil.

This is where your day-to-day diary is of great importance, it is light and portable and can be taken to lectures, libraries etc, amended and added to on the spot. No more re-writing from odd pieces of paper and losing them.

- **Bullet points**

- Always start each action with a bullet point, this will help you to quickly identify the start and end of each task otherwise the sentences will merge into one. Write as neatly as possible. Use this methodology when making notes, writing down actions and writing reports etc. For instance, at lectures it enables you to quickly define where you started and finished, instead of all the notes merging into one long screed, which is not only confusing, but extremely time absorbing when you have to re-read all the notes again.

Hints and practical tips

- By writing "things-to-do" in the place where you know you have the time to do them as and when they occur will save you time. They will be in a safe place where you will not forget the important actions and items and, will ensure you activate the allotted tasks on time. It's a better organised and less stressful way to do things.

- When making notes in lectures etc and for future research to be done or for reading a subject, write down the respective reference such as the book or paper's name, apply the particular reference or research reference that needs to be looked up. It will save you a lot of time!

- To avoid confusion with protracted sentences when writing down the task to be done, try to be as brief as possible, for example:

  - For texting Emma try **TX** Emma,

  - For ringing Emma try **O** Emma,

  - For e-mailing Emma try, **EM** Emma

- Don't be too brief and make it so difficult to understand that interpretation would be like deciphering the Dead Sea scrolls. In the beginning and so you can make quick cross-reference, make out a legend for your abbreviations at the front of your system. Once you are familiar with your own hieroglyphics they will be instantly readable and you will hardly need to cross-reference. Here again this will be a time saver.

- You may want to create a separate tab in your system for example, in the appropriate month page for a special subject you are working on. This gives you a dedicated place to immediately write any information or notes pertaining to that subject and keep them in one place. But remember that any actions coming from this will still have to be written into your to-do's list, otherwise they will remain hidden and will not be communicating with you.

- A written commitment has a better chance of being done than an idle promise.

- If an action cannot be done today put it into a day when you know you have time to do it.

- Keeping your desk, files organised and even the way you approach and do your work should become a habit in itself. A tidy desk is a tidy mind, so make it a practice of keeping your files up to date and desk in order.

- Write down the important things you need to do such as, reading books, library time, writing and reading papers and "time activate" when you want to do them together with their references for ease of identification.

- When first entering "a task" and whilst the various things needed to implement it are still fresh in your mind estimate an approximate time to complete it. Put the time in minutes within a circle at the end of the task. This helps to quickly identify the task when prioritising which is the next step.

- You may want to record your fitness programme at the bottom of the daily page (see example) as an appendage. This could be a means of encouragement.

"Procrastination is the thief of time"
Edward Young, English Poet

Diary Step 3 Fig 3

Fig (3) Examples of: "things to do list"

Typical diary page (with space on right side for tasks to be done)

May   **Monday**   17th

08.00	* Start planning Project X
08.30	* O Mum
09.00	* Look up ref page 5 friday"s lecture
09.30	* Study for papers end week
10.00	* check uni web lecture 12th
10.30	* Lecture Room 51 Block C
11.00	
11.30	
12.00	lunch
12.30	
13.00	
13.30	Library (research)
14.00	
14.30	
15.00	
15.30	
16.00	
16.30	
17.00	* Gym workout
17.30	
18.00	
18.30	
19.00	
20.00	
20.30	* Emma n John Kings Head
21.00	

Exercise point gained today....................Means achieved..............................

Aggregate Points................

Step 4 Stage 1

Organising your diary "Items due from others"

Day Page: Due from others (foot of day page, see example fig 4)

You can record at the foot of the daily page actions and promises that are due from others. For example:

- Email from Emma (eg) Emma EM

- Lecturer's notes due

- letter from bank

- John 2 O me (to ring me)

- Cheque from dad

- Dry cleaning

Here again, brevity is the key but remember not to be too brief!

Hints and practical tips

- When dealing with abbreviations make up a legend for this purpose at the front of your system.

- Don't forget to put them into the day they are due!

- If the data you require from somebody is important and critical to your goals discuss with them what is involved and the probability of it being done by the date you require. This also gives them a chance to think and focus on what is involved before committing. Here in a subtle way you are appealing to their moral duty and commitment which usually works.

- When you choose the date that you need something by try not to make it the very last date, you will leave yourself too small a margin if the deadlines are not made.

- Try to avoid unrealistic deadlines to work to, allow yourself and others plenty of time to do the work in.

- The more you get used to using your system in this way the more you will find this methodology invaluable. Furthermore, it gives peace of mind to the fact that data and information due to you will not be lost or forgotten.

- It enables you to remind others of the promises they made which are due, very important when dealing with deadlines!

Fig (4) Examples of: "due from others"

Typical Diary page (foot of diary day page)

May	
Monday	**17th**

08.00	* Start planning Project X
08.30	* O Mum
09.00	* Look up ref page 5 friday"s lecture
09.30	* Study for papers end week
10.00	* check uni web lecture 12th
10.30	* Lecture Room 51 Block C
11.00	
11.30	
12.00	lunch
12.30	
13.00	
13.30	Library (research)
14.00	
14.30	
15.00	
15.30	
16.00	
16.30	
17.00	* Gym workout
17.30	* Results of prelim exams (see targets)
18.00	* Cheque from dad
18.30	* John promised data on course notes
19.00	
20.00	
20.30	* Emma n John Kings Head
21.00	

Exercise point gained today.....................Means achieved..............................

Aggregate Points................

Step 5 Stage 1

Organising your diary: "Estimating times to do tasks"

When entering a task which will take more than 10 minutes to do, and while the various things needed to implement it are still fresh in your mind, think of an approximate time to complete it. Put the time in minutes within a circle at the end of the task, this eliminates the need for rethinking the task's duration when prioritising your tasks in the next step.

You must not overload your day with items taking one hour plus and if they are of paramount importance then, you have to keep the time clear for you to do them.

Don't attach a time to the small tasks, these usually take on average of ten minutes each. So get used to this when entering tasks.

Hints and practical tips

- Allow plenty of time for doing tasks. Always over estimate the time involved to do a task up to 25%. Allow time between tasks for contingencies and interruptions etc. It will also give you more flexibility in the way you handle interruptions and crisis and therefore you will not feel over pressured with your workload.

- When estimating the duration of tasks, refer to the blocked off times for your appointments and check if you have enough time to do them before committing.

- Items, which you think are important and probably are, may not be important today but will be "number one" tomorrow, so take this into account when planning your day.

- If a task is going to take more than one hour and you don't have the time in that day, break it up into steps of say one hour, book the second hour into the next day. This method encourages you to start the task without the feeling of a mountain to climb or procrastinating.

- Don't cram all the work into one day and impose unnecessary pressure on yourself; by so doing you will end up thinking you have under - achieved which is de-motivating, when in actual fact you have probably achieved quite a lot.

Diary Step 5 Fig 5

Fig (4) Examples of: "estimating times for tasks"

Typical diary page (with appointments)

May	
Monday	**17th**

08.00	* Start planning Project X (30)
08.30	* O Mum
09.00	* Look up ref page 5 friday"s lecture (120)
09.30	* Study for papers end week (30)
10.00	* check uni web lecture 12th (30)
10.30	* Lecture Room 51 Block C
11.00	
11.30	
12.00	lunch
12.30	
13.00	
13.30	Library (research)
14.00	
14.30	
15.00	
15.30	
16.00	
16.30	
17.00	* Gym workout
17.30	
18.00	
18.30	
19.00	
20.00	
20.30	* Emma n John Kings Head
21.00	

Exercise point gained today....................Means achieved...........................

Aggregate Points...............

Step 6 Stage 1

Organising your diary: "prioritising your daily tasks"

Typical daily working page: *(See fig 6)*

1) Your "things to do" list for the day should now be up to date. Choose which tasks are the most important and leading to your goals or targets.

2) Here you take into account the time you have allotted for appointments, you know the time the task will take; now choose the sequence of importance by attaching an alpha letter to them.

During your working day and because of crises, you may have to adjust your priorities, adding to them and in some cases having to cancel or postpone them. At University the transferring of tasks should be to a minimum, as you have a more structured routine. However, when you leave University these new skills will give you a distinct advantage in your ability to deal with your work in the fast moving world you will be in, where changing priorities and demands upon you will be increased tenfold. So, practice this methodology and get into the habit of controlling your workload in a more pragmatic and proactive way so you can deal with the pressures that future positions will inevitably carry.

Hints and practical tips

- When gauging times for tasks, remember to allow a good margin. Should you find yourself finishing early with time to spare you can always proceed to the next day and do some tasks from there. In other words, don't cram all the work into one day and impose unnecessary pressure upon yourself.

- "It is you who is in control of your workload don't let others control you". When new tasks arrive that take priority over others, there is no need to rub all the alpha letters out and start again, just add (1) to the next on your list to be done, e.g. C1 and then add 2 to the current C) e.g. C2. Also challenge why they should take priority before you decide.

- As and when tasks come to mind get into the habit of writing them immediately into the day when you know they can be done and, don't forget to attach their length of time to do them.

- All tasks "due from others" are to be put at the bottom of your daily page, it keeps them in focus and they will not interfere or be confused with your "to do list"

- If you want to keep a record of your fitness programme then refer to the chart at the front of your system. You can keep a daily record in the place provided at the foot of each day.

Diary Step 6 Fig 6

Fig (6) Examples of: "prioritising your daily tasks"

Typical diary page (diary day page)

May
Monday   17th

08.00	(A) * Start planning Project X (30)
08.30	(B) * O Mum
09.00	(D) * Look up ref page 5 friday"s lectu (120)
09.30	(E) * Study for papers end week (30)
10.00	(C) * check uni web lecture 12th (30)
10.30	* Lecture Room 51 Block C
11.00	
11.30	
12.00	lunch
12.30	
13.00	
13.30	Library (research)
14.00	
14.30	
15.00	
15.30	
16.00	
16.30	
17.00	* Gym workout
17.30	* Results of prelim exams (see targets)
18.00	* Cheque from dad
18.30	* John promised data on course notes
19.00	
20.00	
20.30	* Emma n John Kings Head
21.00	

Exercise point gained today...................Means achieved.............................

Aggregate Points...............

Step 7 Stage 1

Organising your diary "Sequencing your priorities"

Typical daily page (see fig 7)

Look at the appointments and see what time is available between the appointments. You already know the time the tasks will take together with their order of importance, so you can now choose when each task can be done. It should be noted here, you should not attempt to do the most important one first when there isn't the exact period of time in the morning to do it. If you do, you may find that it will be all you will do in the day because, with interruptions, restarts etc, the chances of completing your task on time will be severely weakened.

Step A)   Consider which are the tasks that lead to goals.

Step B)   Make sure you have enough time between your appointments, for instance if the lecture room is 10 minutes away and there was only half an hour before the next appointment then you could not possibly attempt a task of an hours duration. Example **B** could be done in the morning and **A** first thing in the afternoon. This method keeps you mindful of their importance irrespective of the time you do them.

Step C)   Bracket the time you are going to do them in the appointment's column together with their appropriate letter. These tasks then become an appointment in every respect.

Hints and practical tips

- Try not to use highlights. If a task is of paramount importance and you have given the subject your due consideration when choosing its priority, then that should suffice. Highlighting can lead to confusion especially when alterations are made.

- Block off the time you need to complete the task with brackets, as you did with your appointments.

- If a task is to take two hours to do and there is not a full two-hour period, break it into two by one hour sessions.

- Don't forget "me time" Leisure time is important, so block off time for yourself.

Fig (7) Examples of: "sequencing your priorities"

Typical diary page (diary day page)

May		
Monday		**17th**

08.00	(A) * Start planning Project X (30)
08.30	(B) * O Mum
09.00	D) * Look up ref page 5 friday"s lecture (120)
09.30	(E) * Study for papers end week (30)
10.00	(C) * check uni web lecture 12th (30)
10.30	* Lecture Room 51 Block C
11.00	(A) (B)
11.30	
12.00	lunch
12.30	
13.00	(C)
13.30	Library (research)
14.00	
14.30	
15.00	(D)
15.30	
16.00	
16.30	(E)
17.00	* Gym workout
17.30	* Results of prelim exams (see targets)
18.00	* Cheque from dad
18.30	* John promised data on course notes
19.00	
20.00	
20.30	* Emma n John Kings Head
21.00	

Exercise point gained today...................Means achieved.............................

Aggregate Points................

Organising your diary: "Working through your day"

Typical diary page: Your daily working page. (See fig 8)

Throughout the working day, always keep your diary with you when you go to meetings, lectures etc. Don't commit information to memory or by writing things down on pieces of scrap paper. This is not good practice, it not only wastes time looking for your notes which also can get lost, mislaid or even forgotten. In consulting your Diary you will instantly see if and when you can do the task or record the idea before it sinks into the subconscious.

Don't forget write "a task" or idea down when it is still fresh in your mind, attach the approximate time it will take to complete in minutes in a circle at the end of your note.

When you have completed a task cross it out it also clarifies the ones you have not completed. This gives you a sense of accomplishment – it's done and behind me feeling – but also allows you to immediately go to the next task at hand. This minimises time wasted in deciding which is next. It should be remembered here that your priorities will not all be consecutive making it difficult to identify them should they not be crossed out.

When other tasks "to do today" crop up and you have time to do them - if they are not of paramount importance- fit them in at the end of your work. Try not to attend to them straight away just because you think they are interesting, this not only distracts you from the subject you are working on but will upset your train of thought.

Through your working day when crises or tasks take precedence over others attach a figure 1 to the task (C1) and then carry on as previously planned.

Hints and practical tips

- Tasks that take a short while usually average ten minutes to do.

- Allow plenty of time for doing the larger tasks. Always over estimate the time involved, also allow time between tasks for contingencies and interruptions etc, it will give you more flexibility in the way you handle interruptions and crises and therefore you will not over pressurise your workload.

- Should you find yourself finishing early with time to spare you can always proceed to the next day and do some tasks from there.

- When you find you are, over or under estimating times, take this into account when you next estimate your task times and allow extra time.

- Remember about 25% of your day can be wasted or used up with interruptions.

Diary Step 8 Fig 8

Fig (8) Examples of: "working through your day"

Typical diary page (diary day page)

May	
Monday	**17th**

08.00	(A) * Start planning Project X	30
08.30	(B) * O Mum	
09.00	(D) * Look up ref page 5 friday"s lectu	120
09.30	(E) * Study for papers end week	30
10.00	(C) * check uni web lecture 12th	30
10.30	* Lecture Room 51 Block C	
11.00	(A) (B)	
11.30		
12.00	lunch	
12.30		
13.00	(C1) (C2)	
13.30	Library (research)	
14.00		
14.30		
15.00	(D)	
15.30		
16.00		
16.30	(E)	
17.00	* Gym workout	
17.30	* Results of prelim exams (see targets)	
18.00	* Cheque from dad	
18.30	* John promised data on course notes	
19.00		
20.00		
20.30	* Emma n John Kings Head	
21.00		

Exercise point gained today.................Means achieved.............................

Aggregate Points...............

Step 9 Stage 1

Organising your diary: "Planning for the next day"

Daily diary page (preparing for next day: (see example fig 9))

This routine should be done on a daily basis at the end of each day as described in Fig 6.

In this step you are planning and preparing your work for the next day. It helps you focus your attention to finish any outstanding items or if this is not possible transfer to the next day. It makes you think, plan and prepare for the tasks you are going to do tomorrow as well as putting them in their order of importance and, more importantly to select the correct time when you can do them in order to get the maximum work done in the most economical use of your time. It will keep you on the course you set yourself and not waste your time in being driven by every circumstance and unscheduled demands you are confronted with. It is all a question of doing the right things at the right time. It eliminates the question when going to bed, "what am I going to do tomorrow?" You will sleep better for it.

These are the steps you have to take.

Step A) Look at the items that have not been done or completed, try to finish them or transfer into the next day or the day when you know you can do them. You should not start a new day with any outstanding work left in the previous day.

Step B) Check that all "due from others" have been honoured. If they have not, either follow them up or if they are vital put them into tomorrow's "things to do list" for action, if not vital put them at the bottom of the page "due from others"

Step C) Think about if there are any more tasks you want to do tomorrow, write them in the "things to do list" for action.

Step D) Bracket the times of your appointments such as meetings, lectures and lunch etc.

Step E) Prioritise all your "things to do"

Step F) Sequence your priorities, remember that if (A) cannot be done in the morning because of time restraints then (B) will be the first to do. This method keeps you aware of their importance.

Step G) Put the sequenced prioritised letters against the time that you can do them and bracket the period of time.

Step H) As and when a task is done remember to cross it out.

Diary Step 9 Fig 9

Fig (9) Examples of: "planning for the next day"

Typical diary page, **with appointments**

May	
Tuesday	**18th**

08.00	(D) * write thesis on for next week (30)
08.30	(E) * Research see notes re lecture last Tues (60)
09.00	(F) * Filing
09.30	(A) (A) * Study for paper end of (60)
10.00	(B) * Shopping food! see list
10.30	* Library re-cap (C2) * Check E-mails etc (30)
11.00	for pm Project X (C1) send em to John
11.30	
12.00	Lunch (B)
12.30	
13.00	Presentation Room 5A (take lap top)
13.30	
14.00	(C1) (C2)
14.30	(D)
15.00	
15.30	(E)
16.00	
16.30	(F)
17.00	
17.30	* Debating society
18.00	
18.30	* Squash Ct Jane
19.00	* Sue Promised copy of her theory - to confer!
20.00	* Match BBC 1 Kings Arms
20.30	
21.00	

Exercise point gained today..................Means achieved............................

Aggregate Points...............
Note! A crisis arrived in the afternoon, you had to send e-mail which took priority over next task eg C becomes C1 etc.

Organising your diary: "At the beginning of each month"

Your month page is for recording targets and goals you wish to achieve and monitoring days in the coming month or if you like for the months ahead as well. These are your "milestones" to keep you focussed on your progress. During the course of time you will have already entered some targets to aim for and projects you wish to start or finish in that month.

At the beginning of each month you can choose the day you want to start and finish them.

1. At the start of each month, turn to your calendar at the front of your diary system (year's overview) transfer any previously made bookings and events into the appropriate space of your daily appointments page.

2. From your month page, transfer to the appropriate day the tasks you have set yourself. For example if there are target dates write down your target's final date. Next, estimate the time needed to complete the work. This will enable you to see it's time span and choose the start and interim monitoring dates. You will also have a better idea of how to do this once you have completed the Targets and Project in stages 4 and 5.

3. Selection of monitoring days. You can achieve this by working from its completion date back to the present, and then you can choose the monitoring dates. You can now confidently put the start date of the project into the appropriate day.

4. Total last month's cash balances and transfer to "drawn forward" account into the coming month. Your cash account page is to be found on the obverse side of the month page.

5. Total up your fitness points gained last month. If you are disappointed, redress this by making a new personal target for this month.

   • Now you have all the "fixed" dates in your daily pages, this now will enable you to plan your other daily tasks around them.

   • This method also will ensure that you are not double booking!

   • It will keep you focussed on the particular goal and targets you are aiming for in the month.

   • You can continually monitor your progress and keep up to- date with the crucial steps needed to obtain your goals.

   • Keeps you informed as to the extent and time you need to invest to achieve your goals.

   • You will not miss target dates when employing this methodology.

Diary: Step 10 Fig 10

Example of: "Using your Month page"

If you have not got one of these pages you could design a simple one on the last day of the month.
These are the primary steps to achieve your goals. Don't attempt too many otherwise they may not be achieved.

Organising your diary monthly page

Write down the things you want to achieve in the month. These will come from the interim steps you are taking to achieve your goals and from the break downs you have made from your larger projects. Also any extra targets and goals which may have been raised in the previous month.

Commit to a start date and when by date. Tick or cross under the asterisk the results. If a cross, transfer to next month and also question why it hasn't been done.

Start date	What I wish to achieve this month	By	*
5 th	* Complete phase 2 (see targets for this term)	10th	√
15 th	* review my areas for improvement (see self assessment page)	20th	X
Start date	Personal	By	*
1 st	Get fit Visit Gym three times a week		√
5 th	Control and budget money better		X

Tips and hints
- *Don't put all the dates down for one day. Allow yourself reasonable time to start and finish each one properly. If you have not completed a task it may be because you are attempting to do too much.*

Your cash account records

At the end of each month you should draw up your cash balances so that you start the coming month with the full understanding of your account status. If you have no facility for this in your diary you can easily design one in the diary or a chart as per example in your XL programme.

(Example) Cash Account: May

Brought forward

Debit £...   **Credit** £..

Date	Item	£	00	Date	Item	£	00

Total £___ _____   *Total £____ __*

Keep score of your fitness and weight records.

Tot up the points you have scored in the previous month. Create a new target for next month, remember a metre every week! If you keep note of your weight, record it each month and set a target to aim for and maintain. You will not know if you are winning or losing if you don't keep score!

Summary of the steps for controlling your diary.

Step1. Organising you personal diary organiser system: "The Calendar"

The Calendar Year. Log all your holidays and important dates so you can see at a glance your yearly and monthly commitments.

Step 2. Your "Appointments"

Make sure all your appointments, such as lectures and meetings, are logged and recorded into the correct day page.

Step 3. Your daily "Things to do list"
Making sure that all the daily and future "things to do" and ideas are recorded in the appropriate day, so they are easily referenced and will be dealt with as and when you want them to and not committed to memory.

Step 4. "Due from others"
Logging and tracking tasks, promises and commitments made to you. Not committing to memory

Step 5. "Estimating the times to do tasks"
Calculating and allowing for he approximate time a task will take to do.

Step 6 . "Prioritising your tasks"
Choosing which is the most important to do in line with your time and goals.

Step 7. "Sequencing your prioritised task list"
Selecting the correct period in which you can to do the task, so you are not pressurised or influenced by other tasks.

Step 8. "Working through your day"

Working through your list of things to do in a controlled and logical way so you can comfortably deal with any crises or interruptions which may occur, therefore ensuring you complete the work you have set yourself to do for that day.

Step 9. "Planning your work for tomorrow"
Starting each and every day with a pre-prepared plan for action and no outstanding work from the previous day.

Step 10. "At the beginning of each month"
Log all your targets, goals and project dates, personal or otherwise for the month. Maintaining up to date record of your cash flow. Keep fit points and records.

STAGE 11

SELF-ANALYSIS

STAGE II: SELF- ANALYSIS

Introduction to self-analysis

When I worked in the United States I was very impressed by the way a colleague was so successful at her work. I asked her what her formula was. She was quite candid and open about it and told me that at the beginning of her career and in order to make any positive progress, she firstly had to recognise the areas where she excelled and, more importantly the areas she needed to strengthen. She had therefore to face up to some fairly serious self-analysis, through a good deal of sole searching, honesty and constructive criticism of herself.

Her very simple approach was to draw a single line down the centre of a sheet of paper. She wrote at the top and left of the line, a plus sign and to its right a minus sign. (see chart 1)

Under the plus sign she wrote the subjects in which she excelled and under the minus sign the subjects that she needed to strengthen and improve. After completing this she realised that unless she made some conscious and positive steps to strengthen her minuses any progress towards a successful career would be seriously impeded. In fact she thought that when she saw the minuses the odds would be too much of a hill to climb and would probably give her a permanent negative attitude. She was determined not to let this control her.

Once my friend completed her self-analysis, she made an action plan through a "route map" (see fig 1) Here she addressed the more serious and salient issues raised under the "minus" sign. She now had the foundation for an action plan to tackle these challenges and make positive steps to improving her career. Furthermore, she added "this had to be supported with a great deal of self-discipline closely coupled with a driving ambition to succeed"

Of course there are more professional and in depth ways for self-assessment, which you will no doubt encounter when seeking a position after university. However, at this early stage of your career this simple method is a quick way for you to understand your strengths and weaknesses more clearly. This way they can be confronted and addressed right at the beginning.

The tools and methods you can employ to deal with these challenges can be made and monitored through the use of your system coupled with a file either manual or in your PC. The main objective here is for you to recognise the areas you need to improve and get them written down as a statement. This is the foundation from which you can build. So start right away by making your own self-analysis. I have set you out an example chart as well as a plain chart for you to work from. When filling it in, be honest with yourself after all, you're the only one who is going to see it.

SELF-ANALYSIS

Chart 1

(Example and suggestion of how you can conduct your own self analysis)

Firstly, write down your name and the date you started the self-analysis.

Putting you your name and the date of entry at the top will give more gravity and purpose to the exercise and act as a datum point to work from.

This is a simple method for your self-analysis. It's an easy way for you to focus on the areas where your performance needs to be strengthened and at the same time recognising your strengths. Write down all your plusses and minuses. Try to be as objective as possible. Be honest, you will not be doing yourself any favours if you're not!

Plusses +	Minuses -
• Writing essays, papers etc	• Balance between work v pleasure
• Research/reading	• Putting things off that I don't like doing
• Keeping in touch with home/friends	• Too many interruptions
• Budgeting finances	• PowerPoint for presentations purposes
• Group debates	• Allowing little time for revision

Note! This doesn't have to be completed all at once. Add to your list as and when the thoughts come to mind.

Chart 2 Self-analysis

Example of how you can conduct your own self-analysis.

In order to proceed in a logical way one has to give careful thought as to the reasons why the minuses have found themselves under this category. This will give you a clearer understanding of the things you have to do to strengthen these areas. Remember "the problem causing the problem"

Transfer all the minuses to the column headed "Subjects for consideration" write down under "rationale" as to why they are there. See example.

Subject for consideration	Rationale
• No balance between work and pleasure	Pleasure is important. Try to catch up with study at week-ends - doesn't always happen
• I put things off I don't like doing	I don't understand the contents So I'll wait until I have time to study it more
• Allow too many interruptions	I like being interrupted - gives me a welcome break
• I want to improve my knowledge of PowerPoint	Never needed to learn the programme
• I need to plan more time for revision	Had not realised the amount of work involved

You have to be honest with your reasons. Don't forget the subject for improvement has been raised as an area you wish to improve. For instance item 3, Interruptions. Most of us don't mind being interrupted and feel it is impolite to repulse an interruption however they can and are a major drain on your time and you have to consider ways in which you can reduce the time spent with interruptions.

Refer to this when filling in your route map which follows.

Route Map

For the areas you wish to strengthen which you got from doing your self-analysis transfer from the headings under minuses to a separate main branch. Consider the order of importance as to how you are going to deal with them, then apply the letter or number as to their respective priority at the end of each branch..

Fig 1

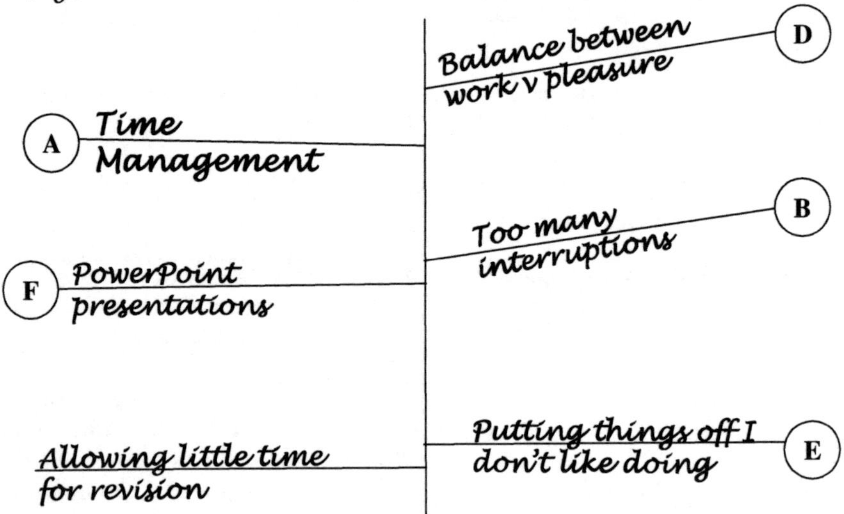

Balance between work v pleasure — D

(A) Time Management

Too many interruptions — B

(F) PowerPoint presentations

Allowing little time for revision

Putting things off I don't like doing — (E)

The following is already sequenced for you. You could add a monitoring date (interim check) After this, the process is as explained under targets and project management

	Start Date	End Date
A		
B		
C		
D		
E		

Route Map

for the areas you wish to improve.

Example of how
you can design a
simple route map
for yourself
Name.........
Start date........

Circle the letter
in order of their
importance at
end of each
branch

Write down start ,
monitoring or check
and end dates, then
record these days in
the appropriate day in
your diary.

Note! Procedure is be
dealt with when you come
to Targets and Project
Management.

	Start Date	Check Date	End Date
A			
B			
C			
D			
E			

STAGE 111

WORKING SMARTER

STAGE III: *WORKING SMARTER*

Economy with the use of your time

Controlling your workload effectively through your diary is the foundation for the platform from which you can manage your targets and projects. It gives you the ability to easily keep track and monitor your targets and projects, whilst also keeping focus on your day to day work. It will boost and maximise confidence in your ability to take on the work and challenges you will be faced with and minimises unnecessary stress and anxiety that will come without this skill. This is the reason why you have firstly to improve your organisation skills through your diary organiser diary .

Before you learned to control and use your diary effectively and done some self- analysis you couldn't have possibly begun to appreciate or gauge the methods, ways and habits that you previously employed to do your work.

In order to make a difference in your work you have to take a closer look at your own methods of working with a view to improving them; it could be regarded if you like as "time study" What do we mean by this? As an example, Henry Ford was the first to conduct a close time study of the methods and ways his production line assembly people worked. He introduced new ways and methods for minimising the efforts and movements of the assembly worker and the order of which parts were supplied and assembled. His findings altered the delivery programme in which sub-contractors supplied their parts and the order with which his own factory made their parts improving cash flow with the right parts at the right time, as well as minimising unwanted and reduced buffer stock. The result was a massive increase in output through a far more economical, efficiently run production line with a vastly improved profitability in the way of manufacturing motor cars. As you can guess after this every other manufacture quickly adopted this method.

You to a lesser extent have to make the same analysis and investigation of your own methods you use to work. This doesn't mean that you are going to be a sort of robot, looking at your watch to time yourself when to do things - far from it. The secret is to work smarter and maximise your output in the most economical way through concentrating on the tasks that lead to goals. A good example of how you can appreciate this more and get a better idea as to how to improve your methods is to look at the Pareto Principle.

Pareto's Principle 80/20 Rule

Vilfredo Pareto. Italian Economist. (1848 – 1923)

Pareto devised a mathematical formula to describe the unequal distribution of wealth in his country, observing that twenty percent of the people owned eighty percent of the wealth. It has been misnamed over the years but many others observed similar phenomena to this rule and have applied the formula such as 20 % of defects causing 80% of the problems. Therefore the Pareto 80/20 rule I think is a good example to help you see a means to improve the way you approach and do your work, and help you manage it more effectively with actions that are really going to make a difference to the results.

Applying Pareto's 80/20 rule to our work can be interpreted in this way, 80% of the rewards you get from your work comes from 20% of your efforts. It gives you a good principle to guide you when deciding the route, approach and execution of your work. Don't misinterpret this by thinking the rest of that time is wasted, it isn't, but you have to think more deeply of how you organise your work. Time is of the essence, and getting the maximum returns from your efforts by working more on the right things; things that are leading to goals - as opposed to doing things right. For example, you can clean up and polish a presentation you are to make in a week's time but it's not the right thing to do when you have to write a paper for tomorrow. It's all about the economy of our efforts the way we plan our work and not wasting our time on things, which are minor or immaterial for the moment. In fact by adopting this methodology you will in the long run, end up by doing less work to achieve the same results.

The danger of not following this procedure is the complete reverse of the Pareto law where 80% of effort will only achieve a 20% result.

How using the Pareto Principle can help you.

Let's try and make some sense of this and see how you can benefit from putting the principle into practice. It's a way of finding out just where your time is being used.

First of all draw a circle. (see fig A) This circle represents the total period of your working day. Write down the headings under the categories that take up your daily workload. It should be noted here when choosing a heading that "study" can be an umbrella for a host of things so try to be more specific when choosing your headings. Note! When choosing headings you have to be completely frank with yourself otherwise it will not be the correct basis to work by and therefore will not be worth attempting. Don't include times for meals, they are permanent where others will be variable.

Examples of headings

- Lectures

- Writing papers

- Dissertations

- Writing thesis etc

- Miscellaneous – such as filing etc.

- Interruptions such as from people, texts-telephones-e-mails

- Research

- Reading

Now try to gauge the amount of time you devote to each heading. Divide the circle into the fractions of the appropriate areas. Write each heading down in its segment of the pie. See example fig A.

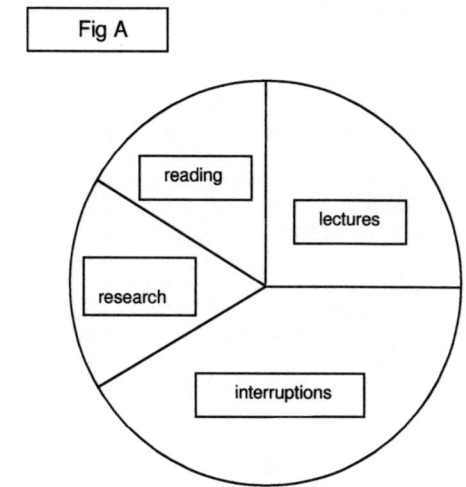

Fig A

Heading

lectures

reading

research

interruptions

Now you can see how your present work is distributed throughout your day. You can also see if and where you are spending too much time on certain items and not enough on others. You can now appreciate where your time is being taken up. The chart clearly shows that interruptions take up a good majority of the day.

Now write down beside each heading the approximate percentage of actual time that each heading you think is taking up.

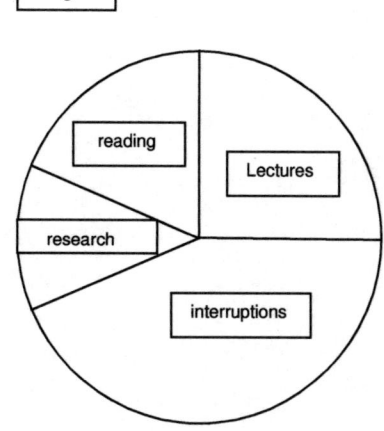

Fig A

Heading	Actual %
lectures	25
reading	15
research	15
interruptions	45

Beside the actual % write desired %. The "desired percentage" is the area - bearing in mind the 80/20 principle - which you have to apply serious thought as to the amount of time you devote to a subject and also consider where perhaps you may be spending more time than you should on another. When considering these areas and taking the Pareto law into account, you may be satisfied that your efforts are being correctly and economically employed.   However, you will also see where you have to make adjustments, where certain segments of the circle have to be expanded and the trivial areas not leading to goals have to be closed up. Give thought to the areas that you need more time for a particular subject. Express these times in their approximate percentage under "desired percentages" This is your new target to work to in order to work smarter.

Figure (A) shows that time is not the main controlling factor. It is what you do with it and how you best employ the time available in the most economical way for the important subjects at hand. In your own chart you will be able to see where your time is being used. You can see where adjustments have to be made in order for your attentions to be directed to the important issues. In the example chart you see that 45% of the day - which is more the norm - is taken up with interruptions. Its good to have some interruptions as they are a light relief from your work as well as a rest and chance to recharge the batteries so to speak. You will always have interruptions and you will never eliminate them all. It would be a very dull world without them but you must not let them control you.

Once you have made your own chart and decided the areas you wish to increase or decrease, reproduce your chart to the new segments that you want to aim for. (see below) For example in the chart we want to increase both reading and research time to 25% and reduce interruptions from 45% to 25 % a net gain of 20% of actual working time.

Heading	Actual %	Desired %
Lectures	25	25
Research	15	25
Reading	15	25
Interruptions	45	25

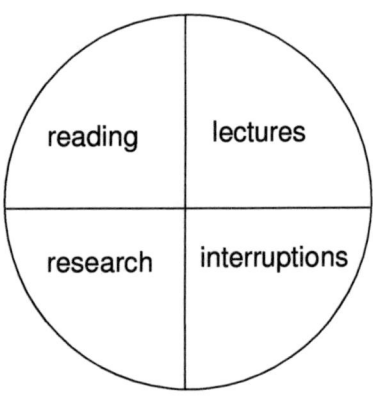

The last example shows the need to reduce the interruption time to 25%; therefore in an 8-hour working day this will still mean you are having two hours of interruptions! So be careful when you are considering the areas you need to increase or decrease. Remember the 80/20 law by making the best use of your time on the subjects that are leading to goals and therefore will make a difference.

Do your own chart as depicted below. In your circle allow plenty of space to write to. If the subjects prove to be too many, make out separate charts for each of them.

When you have written each heading and the time you need to devote to the subject, shade in the areas that you want to expand with the desired percentage. Now you know where your time has been used and where you have to take some positive steps in order to make difference to improve your output , otherwise, you will remain where you where.

Heading   *Actual %*   *Desired %*

_____   _____   _____
_____   _____   _____
_____   _____   _____
_____   _____   _____

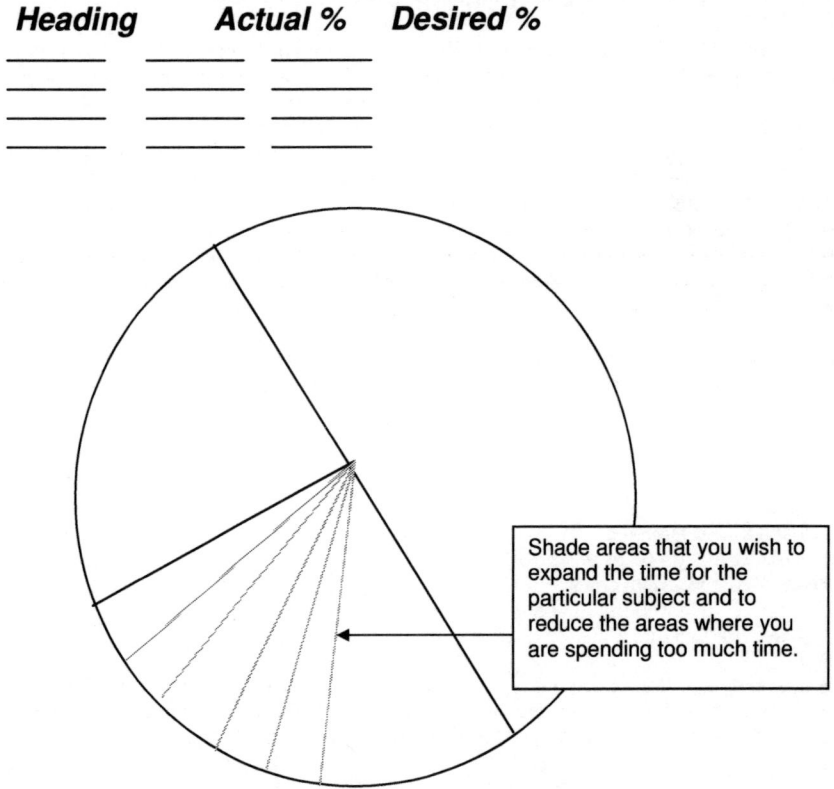

Shade areas that you wish to expand the time for the particular subject and to reduce the areas where you are spending too much time.

The Pareto Principle

Example of how you can strengthen the areas you need to improve.

As the last exercise shows, one of the main things that waste one's time more than any other is being interrupted at our work. We are all guilty of this. It is all too common a practice but it can also provide a pleasant break. However, too much digression from our work is costly in having to catch up for the unnecessary loss of time. If you find you are spending or using up inordinate amounts of time on interruptions and not enough time on subjects that are important then something has to be done about it.

When things are going awry or going off course, you have to ask yourself "Do I really want to go on in this way or, do something about it?" You will see roughly where you are spending your time by using your chart. It will act as a gauge and way to enable you to see where you are going wrong and what you have to do to make the necessary corrections and adjustments to the way you work. Its use will give you a clearer and more defined perspective, a means of taking a step back to see the wood from the trees. Putting the ship back to an even keel. Your chart may show you that you are spending far too much time on one subject irrespective of its importance or not enough on another. Here is the danger of the miss-employment of your time, and this in itself is counter productive and leads to indecision and confusion as to where the real priorities lie. So give your findings some serious thought.

Firstly let us ask ourselves the question as to why we have so many interruptions that waste of our time and what are the reasons that delay our progress? Here are some:

1. Telephone
2. Text
3. e-mail
4. People
5. Unscheduled meetings
6. Meetings that go on after agreed time
7. New data coming in, crisis
8. Computer, allowing our attention to be diverted
9. Study and research time being interrupted

The interruptions listed above are typical of what every person in all administrative based jobs are confronted with every day. You will have recognised and experienced some of them already and the others you will certainly experience in the future.
How do you stop interruptions controlling you? The fact is they will never be eliminated and will always be there but they can be reduced to a minimum. The solution is very simple. You have to make some positive steps in adjusting and modifying the way you do your work and operate, remember Henry Ford? You need to change your behaviour by getting into new habits and disciplines right from the beginning. Once you have acquired these skills they will remain with you as part of your daily automatic routine. Its a small investment to make.

Let's address the above and give you some tips and ideas as how to manage them.

1) The telephone is one of the easiest to control, especially the mobile. It really is a simple case of switching it off during your work time. Any messages can be picked up when finished; and at the time you specify! You have to discipline yourself in this. During lectures you are not allowed mobiles, they would disrupt the whole session. Don't let it do the same to your time.

2) Texting. Here again it's the same as the telephone/mobile. Texts can be controlled, remember you control the texts rather than the other way around. Set some time aside for texting, in your daily programme.

3) The e-mail again is very easy to control. Don't be trapped into thinking you have to look at every one each time they arrive. Set aside time say, in the late morning or at the end of your work. You notice that early morning and afternoon have been excluded because any diversion could take your focus away from the subject you are attending to. It could also put you in a different frame of mind for work and send you in a different direction that you previously set yourself.

4) People are probably the worst offenders for interruptions and lets be fair can also be creators of pleasant interludes as well. It is a question of how you receive the interruption and allow the interruption to happen in the first place. How you deal with people is purely a matter of getting yourself into a habit of conveying to them in a pleasant and subtle manner the way in which you want things to be, especially when you don't want to be disturbed. They will soon get the message and respect you for it; after all it's your time they are taking up. You should not drop everything just because you find something more interesting. You use it as an excuse to stop your work. However, as a majority of interruptions will be from your fellow students, they more than anyone should recognise and appreciate that interruption time should be kept to a minimum. If anybody interrupts me and I cannot spare them the time I simply ask them it we can keep it short or put it off till later. Usually you find the interruption is not that important it was an excuse for them to have a break, however, be careful to respect their time as well as it can work both ways. One of course has to employ a more subtle and non-offensive approach to this, you have to be polite and civilised about it. Sometimes a more subtle approach is through body language. For example if you stand up when someone enters your room it usually signals you want to keep the meeting to a minimum or even that you don't want to be interrupted. A conversation whilst standing is usually far shorter than one made sitting down. If I want to close a conversation I usually get up, this signals, or should, that I want to get on with my own work or I walk to the door and if that doesn't work I bluntly say I really have to get on with my work. Body language can sometimes speak for us. If they haven't got the message by then a good-hearted request for them to leave (in your own language) usually does the trick. Don't let "others" control you. Keeping your door shut with an appropriate notice sometimes works. If someone does burst in after that you have bought the right to tell them so. Be careful about being a anti-social perhaps the notice on your door could be worded; "I don't wish to be anti-social but I am working so please don't interrupt"

5) Unscheduled meetings are one of the most difficult to deal with. They may be and sometimes are very important and necessary. Nevertheless they can be a major drain on your time. You have to work at ways of either, reducing their number or their duration.
When you have had an impromptu meeting that has taken up a good deal of your time ask the initiator to give you more notice before the next meeting. Explain to them you wish to make a more positive contribution by being better prepared, and this can only be achieved by having time for planning and preparing. Also the group as a whole will get more benefit and value for future meetings. If however the meeting is for information gathering or broadcasting suggest that this could be conveyed either by memo or e-mail.

6) Meetings that are protracted. There are a lot of ways of reducing the time meetings take and ways to improve them, but it has to be worked at. If you find that meetings far exceed their closing time, then you have to allow for this when planning your time. You can also put forward as a suggestion at the end of the meeting as from a group point of view, ways in which the meeting can be kept to time. Always try to promote the group. Don't isolate yourself. After all its to your mutual benefit. Ask are the meetings a success? What are the objectives? Maybe there is no agenda or because of unscheduled items – and usually are - that you were not made aware prior to the meeting, that consequently use up the time. At the end of the meeting everybody should comment as to how the meeting went and how and what can be done to improve it. Here are some pointers. Everybody should attend on time. The meeting should start and finish on time. Should the meeting take more than an hour, take a short stretch break, attention and alertness levels start to wane after an hour especially in the early afternoon. If you have a tight schedule to keep and have to finish on time, inform the chair when you arrive of the time you intend leaving the meeting by, there should therefore be little resistance when you do. You have bought the right to leave on time rather than having to make a lame excuse to do so. And if the meeting is run properly and to time there should be no problem. A properly planned and prepared meeting with an agenda where everybody is contributing gives the meeting structure and is conducted in a more satisfactory and professional way. When preparing and planning for a meeting, think about what your input is going to be. What do you want from the meeting? What are your objectives? Always go with the intention of getting something from the meeting. Sometimes ask yourself why are you going and what are you going to be doing there? If you have to chair a meeting and want to finish on time try starting it at 4.30 on Friday afternoon!

7) Unscheduled events. There will always be the unscheduled event, crisis and unplanned circumstances. These in the main are unavoidable, but by allowing for these events in giving yourself approximately 25% extra margin in your tasks (see step 4) These types of interruptions can be easily dealt with and crises kept to a minimum and pass more smoothly.

8) New data. How you receive and deal with new data can be a big time waster. For instance there is always somebody coming in with new information and data to be dealt with and because they think it is important, they place it right in front of you and usually directly on top of your work. It may seem to them of the utmost importance, but it should not be your first priority demanding your immediate attention. Deal with it in the proper way by scheduling it into your priority list as previously described (see step 8 para 5) and it will take its turn. If you drop everything to deal with it you are allowing yourself to be diverted from the task to hand and when returning to it you will probably have to start all over again, spending extra time to bring yourself up to speed.

9) The computer can be one of the biggest time wasters, if you allow it to be. We dive into them emerging hours later having had the most fascinating of journeys but not achieving any of the work you set yourself to do. There are a lot of things in there working very industriously to get your attention and divert you from your set course. The answer to cope with this is self-discipline. You have already pre-planned time to do the work which helps you to hold and keep your focus and eye on the ball to the task at hand and keeping to your objective. Adhere to the course you have set yourself by controlling your work and not letting others control you.

When researching or reading, it's sometimes better to find yourself a quiet spot at the library. Don't tell anybody before hand where you are going. If this is not possible close your door with an appropriate notice to keep out (the actual wording I leave to you) When doing research or whatever don't make it a high mountain to climb. Break it up into sections of say an hour, then have a break or schedule it into the next day. Don't forget how you can jump five metres in a week, a metre per day!

In order to make any behavioural change in yourself you have to change your habit. Distractions are major time wasters and making life for you much harder in having to work longer to catch up. Interruptions upset your rhythm and train of thought, wasting your time into trying to find where you left off and trying to remember where you are, and usually you have to start the subject all over again. Remember, its your time no one else's.

STAGE IV

TARGETS

STAGE IV: Targets

Targeting your goals

Everybody has a goal an objective to aim for. We all have to have our personal "Mission Statement" As well as your overall objective you have already got some targets to aim for from your self -analysis work. These are the necessary paths you have to take to achieve your goals.

You know what your final target is at University. However, to get there you will be making quite a long journey. To make this journey less arduous and more achievable and make steady progress you need to break things down into manageable sized components, so they can be worked through stage by stage.

Targets to aim for are an integral part of our lives. Some targets however, come under the headings of wishes or dreams, most of them are good intentions of which some succeed and unfortunately some fail to become a reality. The reason for some successes in target achievement is when they are instantly measurable and quantifiable and will only take a few steps to complete; this is because they don't need a great deal of planning. The most common reason the bigger targets are not achieved is because they are not properly prepared and planned beforehand. You cannot go on any journey with just a vague sense of direction of where you want to go. The journey has firstly to be mapped out and planned right from the beginning. If you have no firm plan or "route map" there is very little likelihood of them becoming a reality.

First of all, let's start by writing down your own mission statement. You could write this at the beginning of your diary where there should be a name page. Give some thought to it before you commit to paper. Some companies have mission statements because they provide direction, inspiration and a path for their team to follow and aspire to and to achieve the company's targets. Mission statements are a source of encouragement - a standard to focus on - that you will need on your journey through university.

In order to achieve your final goal you have to lay down milestones to navigate your journey. So here again think about the stages you will have to pass through. Write down your targets in your name page at the front of your diary. Remember that some of your short term targets may come after completing your "self-analysis" These obviously are not your main goals but a vital and important step to make to arrive at your final destination. You will also add to these targets as you progress through this training course. Don't be too hasty, initially you might think this is a good idea and start by writing a plethora of ideas and wishes down. Take your time and give them some thought, don't make too many, they must be achievable and don't make for yourself a mountain you cannot climb.

"Yes" I hear you saying, "By the time I have done this I could have done some more work" It's a classic reply from even senior management. The point is, that by becoming more organised you will be able to complete more of the right work, in a more controlled way with less pressure and within the set deadline. Don't go on driving aimlessly into the unknown, you might end up where you don't want to be. It is always best to stop, look at the map to see where you are and where you are going. Taking time in planning your route will improve your chances of arriving on time and in better condition.

Consider your Targets as milestones for your journey. They will provide you with a means for planning and determining a time frame in which to establish deadlines. A means of remaining focused, keeping control and dealing with unscheduled occurrences which, I can assure you will manifest themselves when least expected. Setting Targets assists you in your ambition to succeed and are a very important means to self-motivation. Your self-motivation will need a lot of encouragement and support over the coming years.

Make a route map of all the targets you want to achieve instead of keeping them in mind. This way you will get a more clear perspective of the overall picture as well as the time parameters in which to achieve them. As an example you could make the long branches your long-term goals and the short branches your short- term goals.

Step 1

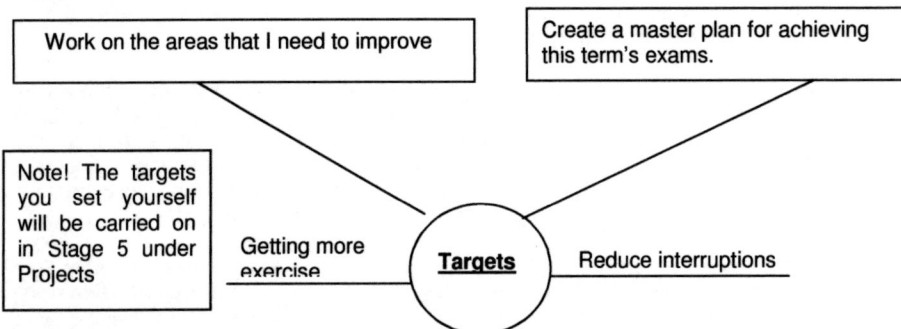

Another target you may wish to set yourself is the very important need for good health which promotes alertness and agility of mind through fitness. Say for example you set yourself a target of 500 points a week. Design yourself a scale of points to be achieved, starting at say 10 points, per mile walked, a full sporting game of two hours could be 200 points etc. By keeping score at the bottom of each day in your diary, you will be able to gauge yourself, and see when you last took exercise. Add them up at the end of the month and write them down in pencil as an aggregate total in the space on your name page at the front or, at the end of each month in your year calendar.

Stage 1V Targets

Route Mapping

Mind mapping is a means for thought provoking. A way to quickly review subjects that you have to address and deal with as well as gathering ideas in a "brainstorming" session. Its a way to raise ideas from deep down in your sub-conscious which need an association of other ideas for them come to the forefront. I prefer to call my particular method as Route Mapping. The method is to create a path or route to achieve a certain goal.

Ideas never come sequentially or in any form of priority. When you are planning something that needs some thought application you normally write down a list, readjust, alter, amend it or strike off the ones which are irrelevant. You then start all over again and come up with another list in no semblance of order of urgency and importance, then after all that work you think of something else to add to the list. This is a big time waster and can sometimes be a de-motivating factor. Route mapping eliminates all of that. It is clearer, uncluttered and allows you to add the associated ideas as and when they arise and be added to the main heading and not lose them in a sea of writing or in your sub-conscience.

Before going on a long journey you must firstly consult a map and plan the route you are going to take, if you are to achieve any degree of success for completing the journey. So consider route mapping as a way of planning and charting your journey of work and studies through University.

When you view the ground from a certain height, you can see all the roads, tracks, junctions, the major obstacles such as towns. You can see your starting point and your destination. You can see the challenges that lie ahead. That doesn't mean that your journey will be all smooth going, there always will be crises to deal with, but at least a properly charted route will ensure you can remain in control and deal with the surprises in a more proactive way. Route mapping will enable you to see where you are, you can fix targets, review and monitoring dates. This is the overall view that you need before the start and during any journey. It will not foresee or predict problems or the inevitable crises you will encounter. But it will give you the flexibility with your planning to be able to cope with them. How to deal with these will be addressed later. In the beginning you have to map your journey and this is the way you do it.

The main branches of your route map are the main roads as to where you want to go. The branches off, are the various junctions, side roads, intersections and hazards which help you navigate your course. The numbers you apply as priorities are like the milestones of your journey. For example, if you start with a subject such as the Semester facing you, you will have to organise and plan your work time, the subjects involved, study time, library research, papers to be written even shopping and all the other challenges facing you.

Instructions for using a Route Map (fig 1)

1) On your main branches write down the salient points and headings, which you want to address and attend to. This doesn't have to be completed all at once, it can be added to, modified or taken away as and when the idea or subject comes to mind.

2) Add side branches for the various tasks and actions necessary and important to plan a route and means to achieve the desired result.

3) At the end of each main branch, write the appropriate letter or number in their order of priority or sequence to the tasks on the side branches so as to give you a list of the order of which you want to do first.

4) Draw a straight vertical line below, and write down the amount of letters of the main branches with the lines straight across the vertical. (See Fig 1)

5) To the right hand side at the top of the vertical line write, start date, consider very carefully when you have got to finish it by and add an end date. (see fig1) This will then give you the time that's involved to achieve your aims. Now you have charted your course, these will be the "milestones" for your journey; you can now write these "milestones" down in your daily pages in your diary or, if they have to be done until next month, enter them into next month's monthly page.

Hints and tips.

- Route mapping is a way to keep focussed on your priorities. Use it as a means to find a path forward.

- Use route maps at lectures and meetings.

- It is a means of thought provoking and raising ideas from the subconscious.

- Use it when you have to decide a path for your workload.

- Use them in brainstorming sessions when groups are involved and where ideas have to be raised and shared with others. When deciding a common policy and agenda. For this purpose I suggest you use a flip chart everybody can see at a glance the route map. You will be surprised how quick it will raise ideas and get everyone involved.

- If you find one heading demanding more space on one route map, start another route map under the other headings.

Route mapping will keep you focussed on your priorities instead of wasting effort on minor and irrelevant subjects, which only erode your time and let you stray away from the path of your intended goal.

Route Map

For the areas you wish to strengthen which you found when doing your self-analysis, transfer from the headings under minuses to a separate main branch. Consider their order of importance, then apply the letter or number as to their respective priority to the end of each branch.

Fig 1

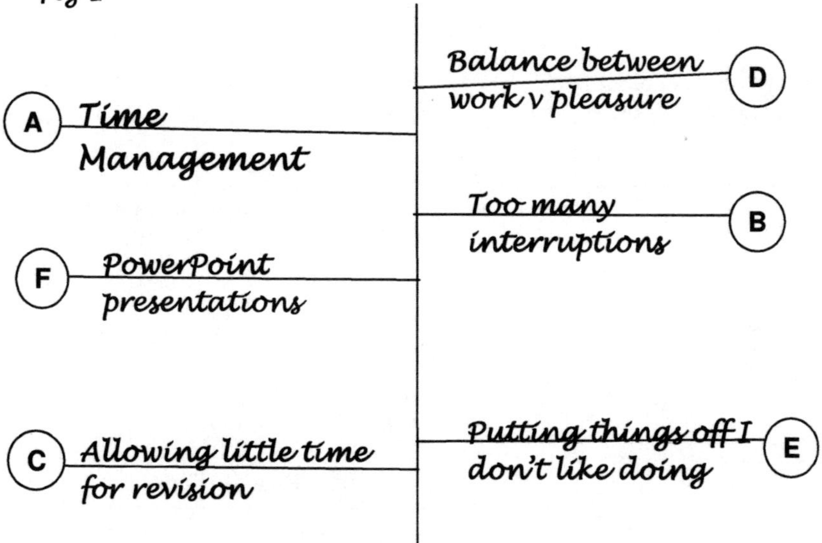

(A) Time Management

(F) PowerPoint presentations

(C) Allowing little time for revision

(D) Balance between work v pleasure

(B) Too many interruptions

(E) Putting things off I don't like doing

Write down the letters as per example so they are sequenced. You could add a monitoring date (interim check) After this, the process is as explained under project management

	Start Date	Check	End Date
A			
B			
C			
D			
E			

Route Map

for the areas you wish to improve.

Here is a plain example for you to copy Always write your and start date.

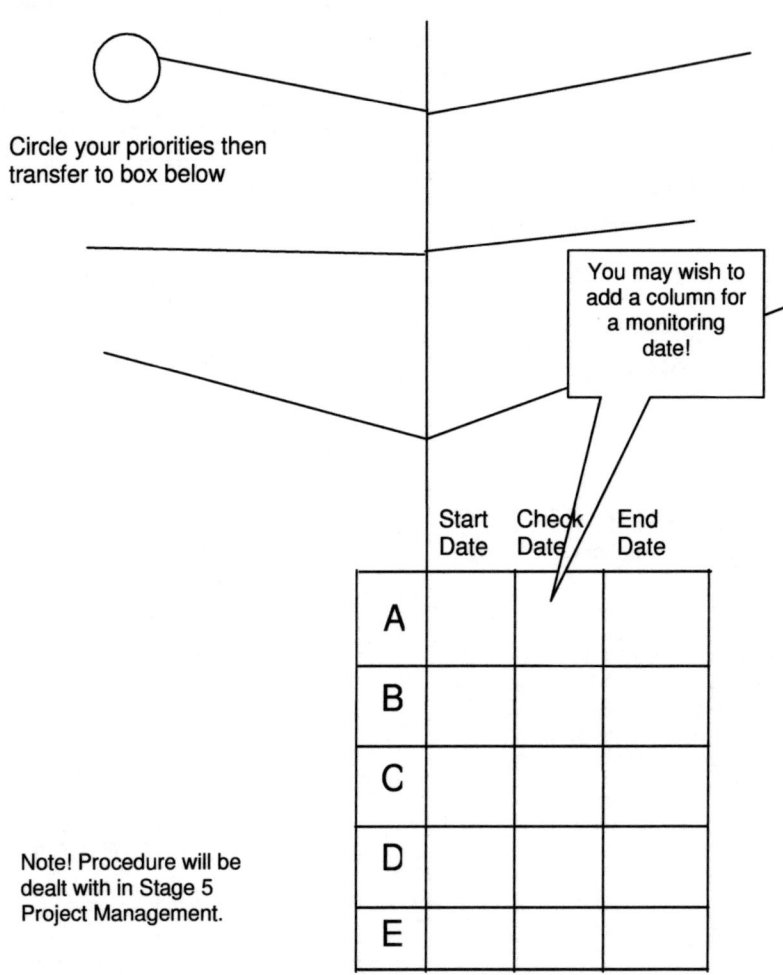

Circle your priorities then transfer to box below

You may wish to add a column for a monitoring date!

	Start Date	Check Date	End Date
A			
B			
C			
D			
E			

Note! Procedure will be dealt with in Stage 5 Project Management.

STAGE V

PROJECT MANAGEMENT

STAGE V: PROJECT MANAGEMENT

One of the reasons why projects are not completed on time or concluded only after a very fraught period of grief, frustration extraneous hours of stressful work and exhausted nerves is because we fail to start them on time. Why? There are many quite plausible excuses and reasons made as to why they are late, but, in the end it comes down to the fact that we have not properly prepared and planned them in the first place. If we don't completely understand what is involved we tend to "wing it" from day to day. We procrastinate. We put things off because of our fear of the unknown. It is all because we simply have not taken a proper look at what is involved. Once we do, it removes the fear because we know what has to be done and the route we have to take. Here are some of the many reasons that are used for not starting and finishing on time

.

- Lack of information.
- Change of priorities and altering of specification and deadlines
- Poor understanding of subject matter
- Not enough time
- Unclear time scales
- Difficulty with estimating time to do work.
- Delay in information from "others"
- Unscheduled meetings and meetings that overrun
- Task seemingly too big.
- Poor preparation
- emails, texts
- The end dates are far away so there is seemingly no hurry.
- We procrastinate and put off "picking up the ball"
- We even find excuses to justify procrastination.

We should not lose sight of the big picture but we also have to keep the smaller picture in focus as well. It's impossible to navigate a car from a 1000 ft. It is important to see the big scene but from that height the smaller diversions, road works and traffic lights, obstacles etc are indefinable. You have to be in the driving seat to negotiate the hazards of your journey, be able to cope with breakdowns, stoppages, delays and diversions in order to be arriving on time with safety. We need to control matters from the ground as well as having the ability to view the overall scene form a higher perspective.

What is a Project?

In business terms a project has a start and end date. It is drawn to a satisfactory outcome by successfully controlling and organising materials, money, time and personnel.

This definition covers almost any project there is, from a hydroelectric dam to making a simple broom to sweep the floor. The fundamental differences which separate projects with all the other aforesaid reasons is that projects have a start and an end date. A project isn't necessarily a large and protracted undertaking. Other jobs for example the postal service, is a process. In the first instance it may have been a project. New structures or innovations to its management may be a project but the day to day service is an ongoing process, which ostensibly has no end date.

The work you are doing will come under the category of "Project" after all there are time limits and, a definite end date. It will have materials, the need for organisation and the control and management of work together with targets and objectives as well as a certain amount of monetary restrictions, although the latter is not a big criterion here. However the incorporation of all these skills will assuredly play the major part for you to achieve your goals.

Firstly you must consider the project/s you are embarking upon; what are the challenges and expectations and more importantly their time frames. You must not lose focus of the overall objective. What I mean by this is, that if the end date is in 18 months time you may choose, due to its long duration, to shelve it in your mind with the idea that you will return to it when the time draws nearer. If you do, the danger here is that you could get fixed with "tunnel vision" on a single subject. You must remain aware and recognise the milestones on your journey. In order to properly evaluate time scales and more importantly what has to be achieved within that time it is therefore imperative you attend to them right from the start and not put them to one side.

Here is a reliable means by which you can analyse your projects, by breaking them down into modules and manageable components, quantify your workload, set targets, review days and checkpoints so as to keep track and monitor each subject. Here, you can calculate for and write in contingency margins so as to expediently meet and deal with crisis as and when they arrive, thus lessening the time with reactive management and becoming more proactive.

IN THIS STAGE OF PROJECT MANAGEMENT YOU WILL BE COVERING THE FOLLOWING AREAS:

1) Project review and defining your projects.

2) Prioritising the order in which to control them.

3) Route mapping, breaking them down into modules and manageable components.

4) Strategic planning

5) Goal and target setting

6) Tracking and monitoring

This is a way of simplifying your project right from the beginning by mapping out its basic routes and installing milestones for the journey. By this means you will always have a route map to refer to which allows you to keep track and continually monitor your progress. If you wish you can set these project planners up in your PC under an exclusive file bearing the project's name. Whichever way you choose to do it you will be able to keep track of them through the diary.

Reviewing your projects

Without good Time Management skills you could not proceed with project management in a confident and positive way.

Which project to do first?

Firstly you have to get the complete picture of how many projects you have to do. Remember to focus on the ones you have for this period, it will keep matters in perspective. You have to prioritise the order in which to do them. This exercise should be done at the beginning of each semester and reviewed and recorded on the relevant monthly page.

So let us start at ground level. Firstly write down the main Projects you are going to do this Semester and also write in their end dates. If you wish, this can cover other activities you are participating in but keep them to a minimum so as not to distract from the main purpose of the exercise.

(Fig 1)

Here is an example and suggestion of a simple graph of how you can record the Projects you have to complete

Project name	End date
Project A	
Project B	
Project C	
Project C	

Planning and preparing your Projects

What you may think is an easy and simple scheme to organise is not what it may seem in the first instance. Once you have mapped out the bare skeleton of what you have to do, considered and investigated what is involved in workload, input and time   sometimes turns out to be quite complicated and confusing. You write copious lists and re-write them ending up with a confused sheaf of papers, its very time consuming.

A properly organised event whatever it is has a better success rate than one that is not planned. Furthermore, being properly prepared you are in a better position to control, adjust, alter and correct matters when things go wrong or unexpected happenings happen
.
Here is a simple straightforward way to analyse and elaborate upon a subject and be able to observe it with a birds-eye view without the need of copious notes.

The chart that follows is designed to allow you to prioritise your projects and acts as a permanent indicator for them. As a paradigm I have chosen a subject we can all identify with, which is holidays.

Again a route map is being used. Here there are six main points to consider. There are many branches to consider when organising a holiday. However, if for example a single subject needs extrapolation or contains a lot of sub headings to deal with then you can create a separate route map exclusively for it.

Suggestion for your Project chart

Create a large chart and put it on the wall near your desk as permanent reminder.

Write down the main branch titles in order of their priority when you have done your route maps (next pages) together with their end dates.

	Project Name	Start date	Review date	End date	Comments
1					
2					
3					
4					
5					

The Route Map for Project: Holiday

You will be by now, familiar with the route map. Over the next pages are step by step examples of creating the basic routes and agenda for a simple project.

Step 1)   When you know the order in which your projects are to run (Fig 3 previous page) assign each project to their own separate "route map" together with their respective titles. You will also have determined their end dates so write them down as well.

Fig (1)

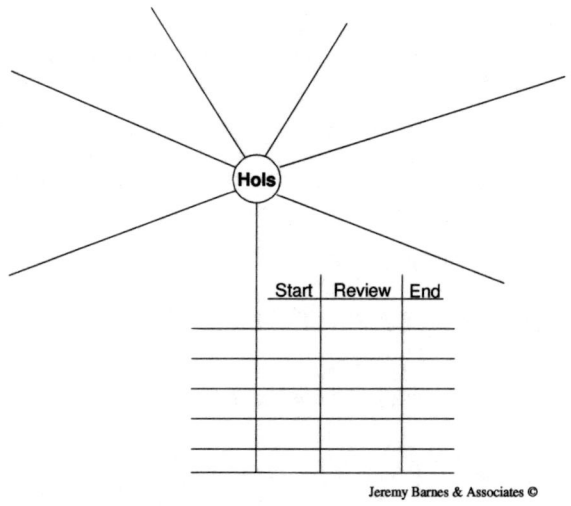

• Fig 1

Notes

Tips

You can run more than one Project at a time so long as you record their respective start and end times in your diary system; this is why it is also a good idea to display them on a graph beside you.

Step 2) You will see there are four branches to our route map. These will formulate the agenda. You can add to them if you wish but make sure you allow plenty of space. Your project will fall into various categories or modules so start by writing their headings along each main branch.

Fig (2)

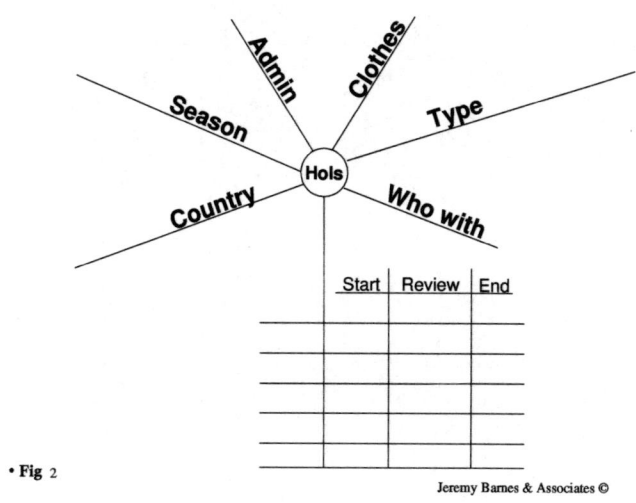

• Fig 2

Jeremy Barnes & Associates ©

Notes:

Tips
• If you find the need for more main branches, create a separate route map, to run beside the first one. For quick identification, after their titles, affix A & B etc.

Step 3) Write down the subheadings of the tasks to be done in order to complete their respective main branch heading.

Fig (3)

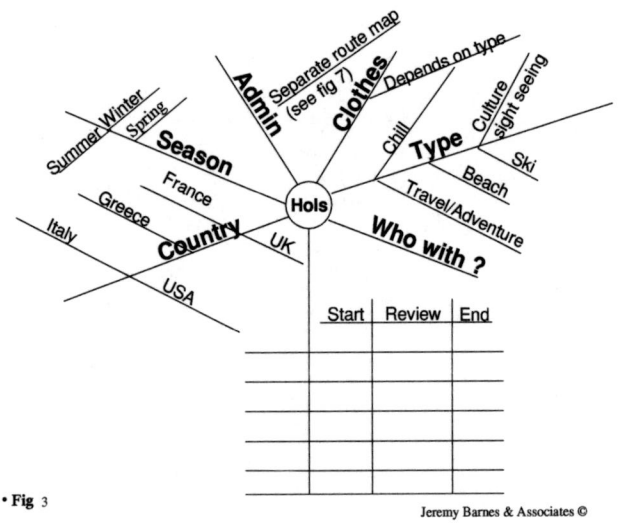

• Fig 3

Notes:

Tips
- Tasks and ideas never come sequentially. If you find you are stuck for ideas and the things that are needed to be done, firstly, write down the ones that you know are to be done and by so doing this will jolt the mind and trigger more. If you cannot add to them you can always refer to them a later stage. The point is to get the initial points downloaded from ones mind.

Step 4) Think about the order in which you need to finish the main headings and write their order down in a circled letter at the end of each branch.

Fig (4)

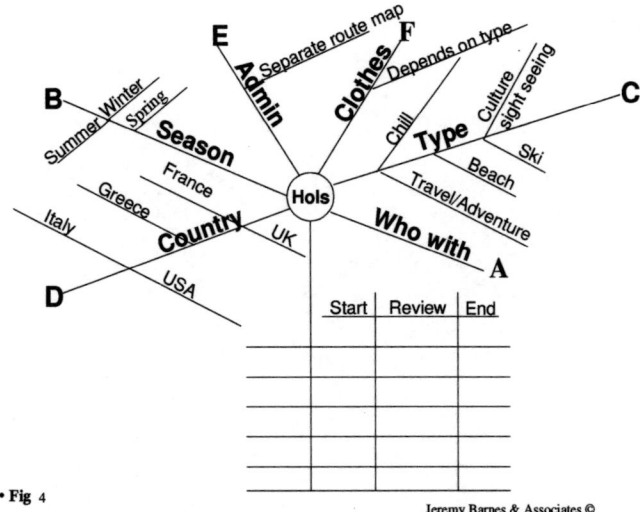

• Fig 4

Jeremy Barnes & Associates ©

Notes:

You will note here that when choosing the sequence for priority (A) I have obviously selected the title "who you are going with". If for instance you choose to go with a group or, just another or by yourself the route map will act as the basis for discussion and elaboration which can be easily read by all parties so that you can all arrive at your deliberations more quickly.

Tips
- If you find that because of equal importance, two main branches will require to be worked on simultaneously, don't dwell on the decision too long, you have to start one of them first, the other will follow as they then can run in parallel. The main point here is that wrestling over the decision will unnecessarily delay and confuse.

Step 5)   You might also plan the order of how you are going to do the sub - branches as well and, for ease of recognition it is better here to use numerals.

Fig (5)

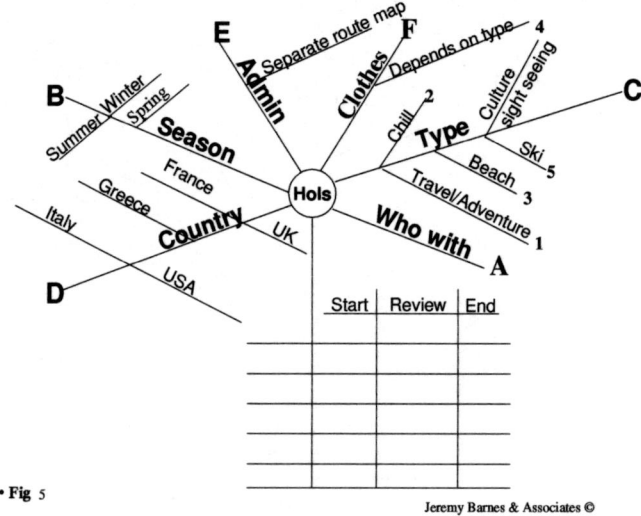

	Start	Review	End

• **Fig** 5

Notes:

Tips
- Don't forget that if you find the route map is getting crowded, create another route map by splitting above in half, starting at A to C and then D to whatever, and not forgetting, to re-affix A & B to each of their titles.

Step 6) Once you have completed the above, write the main headings down in their correct order in the rows below.

Fig (6)

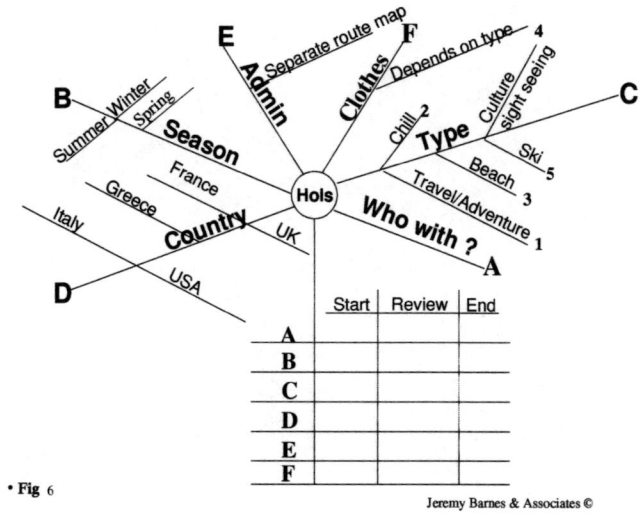

• Fig 6

Notes:

Tips
- Note that (F) depends on the type of holiday you will choose, so its dependant on (C) & (D) You will meet this type of dilemma with your own projects but in viewing them in this way it will help you in your decision making.

Step 7)   In step (6) under the main branch title Administration, because of the intensity of its data, a separate route map was to be created. Here is an example of that.

Fig (7)

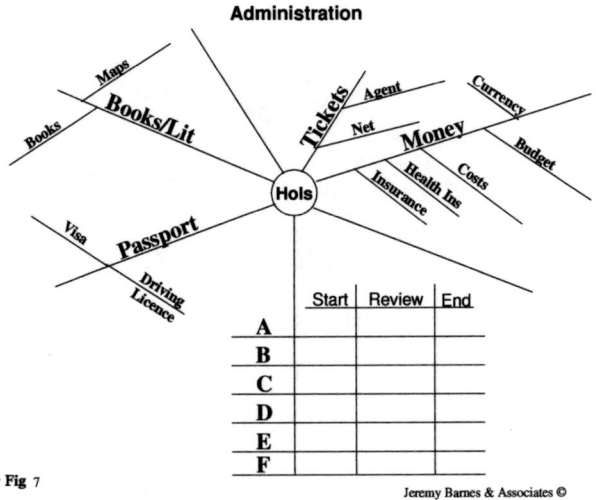

• Fig 7

As an exercise, choose for yourself how you would prioritise the tasks for this.

Notes

Step 8) Now you know the order in which you are to proceed with your projects write down their start dates in the box below

Fig (8)

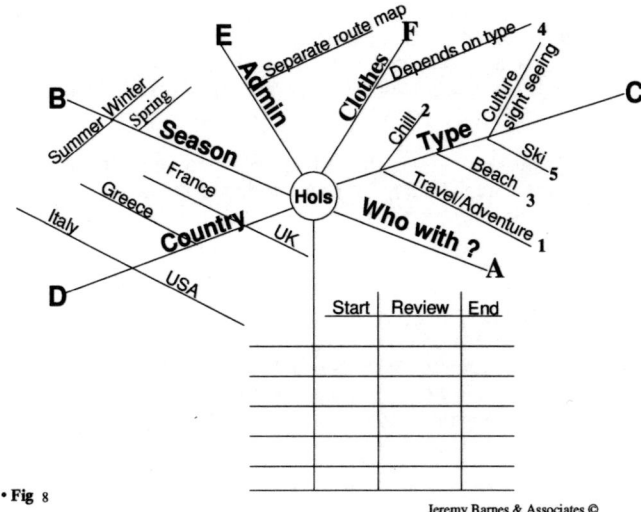

	Start	Review	End

• **Fig** 8

Notes

Tips

- The best way to find a start date of a project is to work from its end date and work backwards. Keep consulting your diary to check if there are any conflicting dates. During this time it will become evident of the level of intensity of work needed, therefore there should be no surprises.

Step 9) Record the start and end dates in the appropriate day of your diary, you may wish to make a note of them by putting them in your calendar, but keep only to the big events in your calendar otherwise too many will merge and therefore become confused.

Step 10) At this step you determine your review or monitoring days, these dates too should be recorded in the appropriate day of your diary. You may consider some of them of no great importance at this stage, however, when these dates come up as reminders and gentle nudges you will benefit from them in the long run. Don't commit them to memory always write them down so as to keep your mind clear for the really important issues.

Step 11) Once your projects have been planned you can then start to record the various day to day actions needed and the monthly review days all as described in the beginning in stage 1.

You now have the whole time frame of your workload. Not in intricate detail, that's for you to fill in your main plan, but you now have the routes and milestones to guide you in how you are going to tackle each project. Remember that sometimes it is better to slow down before you can go at full speed. This exercise will not take a long time but it is a way for you to analyse and determine the route you are taking and prepare for your journey.

"Don't turn a problem into an obstacle or make an obstacle into a problem"

Here are some examples and suggestions for you to copy to record your goals and targets. Keep this in your diary or personal computer, XL?

My Goals and Targets

Name ....

University ....

Reading .... *Entry date* ....

My Mission Statement. By this date......... I Will...........................

Target.........................By date............... Review date ....

(Add as many review dates as you wish but remember to record them in your diary as you do with the start and target dates.

═══════════════════════════

Mid Term Exam Date .... *Results* ....

Areas for improvement after mid term results ....

1st Year exam date .... 1st Year exam results...........................

Areas for improvement after 1st year exam results ....

2nd Year exam date .... 2ndYear exam results.........................

Areas for improvement after 2nd year exam results......................................

Make out a route map and plan how you are going to improve your performance (if the need arises) Refer to stage 2 Self-analysis

═══════════════════════════

Target for keep fit exercises, games, sport etc for accumulated points per month

I am going to achieve each month............points Aggregate points.........................

Weight ....Date.........Target Weight............ By Date.................................

(Choose how many points you want to award yourself say per game per hour or

per mile run. Always keep score then you'll know if you are winning!

═══════════════════════════

Here is a typical exam monitor format that you may wish to copy for you diary or XL.

Module	Coursework	%	Exams date	%	Total

Summary and conclusion

Don't revert into the old bad habits. When matters are proceeding well you may become complacent and can easily be side-tracked and forget the early disciplines learned. This is usually because you have not practised your new skills enough for them to become a habit. So, when things don't go well remember how well they originally went and why the new methodology worked for you at the beginning! Don't forget, you can always stop, put the handbrake on and take time to study your map and re-establish where you are and more importantly where you are going! It is better to slow down before you can speed up, otherwise your journey will take longer than you may have time for.

Here are some reminders to help you.

- It could be that you are attempting to do too much by cramming all your tasks together. Spread your work evenly, if you finish early you can always start tomorrow's work.
- Take time to plan your work
- Underestimating the time needed to do your tasks only puts unnecessary pressure upon you.
- Allowing too many interruptions from "others" is a big time consumer also respect other people's time. Don't let others control your time
- Allow 25% extra for contingencies such as interruptions and unforeseen crises.
- Don't procrastinate with indecision and putting off what can be done today. This also includes forward planning for your main project and targets not just the day to day tasks
- Do the more difficult tasks first, the rest will be done more quickly; and keep sequencing tasks in their proper order of importance or, within the time available.
- Remember at all times to remain focussed on your main objectives. You will have set these out as "milestones" in your monthly page. Continually monitor your own performance and progress, don't ignore them and let them drop out of sight.

If you choose to keep any records for sport or your exams in your PC always record the dates when you want to monitor them in your diary, so you don't lose sight of them
.
Finally as I say to all my delegates at my workshops "keep taking the tablets" they will work in the end. Good luck. I wish you every success not only in achieving your Degrees but also, with your future career.

"The true art of living in the world is more like a wrestler' than a dancer's skill. Whatsoever falls upon you, be prepared so that nothing may overthrow you or cast you down."

"Meditations"
Marcus Aurileus. Roman Emperor